D0539727

ONLINE
JOB
HUNTING

100574298

The authors would like to thank the following for their vision, commitment, support, encouragement and assistance in the creation of this book. Jon Finch, who saw the sequel fully developed in his mind even before I did. The team at Kogan Page, who give the lie to the belief that writing is a solitary pursuit – this book would not have come to you without the tireless efforts of Helen Moss, Tom Hickman, Fiona Meiers and especially Martha Fumagalli who 'worked the clock' to get media events to happen in the UK, regardless of where we were in the world.

In the United States, we would like to thank our dear friend Heidi Garrett just for being who she is and – saving the best till last – our research team, led by the indefatigable Dianne Eisenhardt, and her interns in Jamestown: Eleanor Spritzer and Nora Dumplemeyer. In Jamestown, Terra would especially like to thank Tiffany Krihwan, and in New York I'd like to say a word of thanks to My Man Godfrey, who was with me every moment of producing the book. Thank you all so much for making this book a blast!

WITHDRAWN
FROM THE LIBRARY OF
UNIVERSITY OF ULSTER

ONLINE JOB HUNTING

GREAT ANSWERS TO TOUGH QUESTIONS

MARTIN YATE & TERRA DOURLAIN

KOGAN
PAGE

100574298

650.
14
YAT

First published in 2001

Apart from any fair dealing for the purposes of research or private study, or criticism or review, as permitted under the Copyright, Designs and Patents Act 1988, this publication may only be reproduced, stored or transmitted, in any form or by any means, with the prior permission in writing of the publishers, or in the case of reprographic reproduction in accordance with the terms and licences issued by the CLA. Enquiries concerning reproduction outside these terms should be sent to the publishers at the undermentioned address:

Kogan Page
120 Pentonville Road
London N1 9JN

© Martin Yate and Terra Dourlain, 2001

The right of Martin Yate and Terra Dourlain to be identified as the authors of this work has been asserted by them in accordance with the Copyright, Designs and Patents Act 1988.

British Library Cataloguing in Publication Data

A CIP record for this book is available from the British Library.

ISBN 0 7494 3646 8

Typeset by Saxon Graphics Ltd, Derby
Printed and bound in Great Britain by Clays Ltd, St Ives plc

Contents

Martin Yate is an internationally best-selling author. He has held major posts as a director of training and personnel for several international companies. His best-selling title *Great Answers to Tough Interview Questions* (also published by Kogan Page) is now in its fifth edition.

Terra Dourlain has over 12 years' experience in human resource management and employee development. She currently runs a career services company, which specializes in career counselling and CV writing, and also conducts seminars on Internet search strategies.

Introduction

You are ahead of the crowd when you implement an online job hunt. While millions of companies have rushed to establish their Web sites and use them for recruitment purposes, the majority of tradition-bound UK workers have stated unequivocally that they have no intention of ever going online.

Employers today are looking for a new kind of worker to put on the corporate fast track, someone who is technologically adapted. Computer technology has changed the entire world of work, from the very structure of companies to the make-up of the jobs themselves. Whole job categories have disappeared, those responsibilities now being executed entirely by computer. Other jobs have been simplified beyond belief, giving opportunity to workers with less education and fewer skills; these jobs pay poorly and offer few opportunities for professional growth.

A third group, however, is poised to benefit significantly from these workplace changes. This group comprises those people who have embraced technology and harnessed it for the improvement of their personal and professional lives. For these are the professionals all employers seek for key growth positions at all levels within their corporate structures.

Employee recruitment is all about weeding out job candidates. The CV (or résumé) is an example of this weeding-out process in action. Without the CV an employer would have to interview every single job candidate. The result is that no real work would ever get done. Enter the CV – now

an executive can sit and speed-read through 30 CVs in as many minutes, probably weeding out 95 per cent of them.

The Internet has come as another valuable tool in this recruitment and weeding-out process. If a company wants to recruit selectively only the technologically adapted for certain positions, what better way to do it than to use a recruitment vehicle that only the technologically adapted can use in the first place? Consequently every company that hopes to be competitive in the 21st-century global marketplace is using its Web site, and thereby the Internet, to weed out the technologically retarded.

The thinking is simple: 'If you can't use a computer and don't understand the World Wide Web, you won't waste our time because you won't even hear about these jobs.' In the UK, a major survey recently identified that the majority of people have absolutely no intention of ever using the Internet. This is just excellent news for someone like you. It means that when you apply for jobs online you are immediately setting yourself apart as one of the new breed of desirable professional, while at the same time reducing your competition for that job by your very approach.

Now by technologically adapted we don't mean the ability to write computer programs or design your own Web site. The fact that you haven't broken out into a cold sweat on picking up this book is signal enough that you probably have what it takes to compete in this New World. Probably? Well, that's why you got the book; once you have finished it, you will absolutely have what it takes and be able to do it.

Together the authors have over 40 years in the career field and have been using the World Wide Web as a job-hunting and career management tool since its very inception in the early 1990s. We are not Web Weenies; we just recognize the potential of this new communications medium to transform, not only this particular job hunt, but all your future job hunts and your complete career management strategy as well.

Most people don't even have a career management

strategy. They go from one job (when they can't stand it a moment longer) to the next available job, essentially jumping out of the frying pan and into the fire.

With the tools we will give you within these pages, you will not only get a far wider range of professional opportunities for this job change, but you will also learn how to keep a constant eye on the employment marketplace. You will have the ability to be more effectively proactive in future job hunts. You will be able to think ahead about what your next logical step up the ladder of career success should be and, having decided that, have the capability constantly to scan the horizon for opportunities that fit your professional needs. Such ability has never existed before. Now it is at your fingertips.

Now let us tell you how to use this book. *Online Job Hunting: Great answers to tough questions* is specifically about how to use the World Wide Web in your job hunt. We are not going to confuse you with technical jargon, and neither are we going to waste your time trying to give you a degree on the workings of the Internet. After all, you don't need a degree in engineering to drive a car.

Each chapter in the book is designed to give you a new tool to use in your job hunt. We explain the challenges that make such a tool desirable; we then describe the tool and show you how to use it in your job hunt. By the end of the book you will have an arsenal of highly effective job-hunting weapons and the strategies with which to implement them most effectively. These will be tools that you can use for a lifetime.

On this note we should mention that the online world is a volatile place that is in an ongoing state of evolution. There are and will be changes in this world from year to year. Sites will come and sites will go. New technologies will arise that make new tools possible. For example in the United States, where things are somewhat further along, there are exciting job-hunting tools available that don't as yet have a UK application. Yet these tools will be with us soon, so the online job-hunting picture will change. Consequently, we

will be updating this book on a regular basis to keep you abreast of all the latest tools, ideas and tricks, just as Martin has done for years with *Great Answers to Tough Interview Questions* (published by Kogan Page).

But for starters we concentrate on getting you that next job as quickly and efficiently as possible. Online job hunting is new for everyone in the world right now, so we are not making many assumptions. What we are taking as given is that you have a CV and some basic computer skills, and that perhaps you have surfed the Web once or twice; that is all we are assuming.

Even if you have never logged on in your life, this shouldn't be a problem. Just find a friend, neighbour, colleague or any 14-year-old, and in less than two hours you will have an elementary grasp of this brave new cyberworld. That is all you will need to start; given this minimal base knowledge, you have everything you need to learn and implement the valuable lessons in this book.

Because the entire online world is like a booming Wild West town, things are in a constant state of change and turmoil. Sites will come and go; sites will boom and bust; sites will boom and be bought or merged. We have identified over 1,000 great career sites for you in the book, 1,001 to be exact.

We literally spent months visiting sites, using them, watching them grow and change. We searched for sites for everyone, new graduates to executives, sales and marketing, accounting, engineering, education, retail, medical, social services – you name it, we uncovered sites specifically for you. We did this to give you a head start – but we made it an appendix (Appendix A), because the information and advice we offer in the chapters is your foundation. Finding sites for you won't do you any good if your CV and cover letter are not up to par. So pay attention to the whole book and not just the 1,001 great sites listed in the back.

One last word of advice on how to get the best out of *Online Job Hunting: Great answers to tough questions*: use a highlighter as you read it. We have written the book with a

couple of firm precepts in mind: first, not to waste the reader's time with padding but to get to the point and make that point crystal clear; and second, to give actionable advice on every single page.

Of course, we don't know which particular bit of advice on each page will ring bells in your mind, which is why we recommend the highlighter. This is a practical 'how to' book that you will also use as a reference vehicle, so using a highlighter will enable you speedily to locate nuggets of help that you recognize as particularly applicable to your situation.

Now let's get down to the business of an effective online job hunt.

one

What is online job hunting all about?

Just what is the Internet or the Web, and how can it help me in my job hunt?

So you need a better job with a brighter future? As a smart, modern professional you want to stack the odds in your favour, so you talk to friends who've been through the process recently; you've heard about the Web and you wonder how it might help you in your current job hunt, with all its special circumstances.

Any job hunt is a pain where a pill can't reach; after all, it's not as if many of us have a wide frame of reference for successful job-hunting techniques. So why would you want to complicate an already confusing challenge by investing precious time to learn all that online voodoo when there is no general acceptance for the approach?

Why? Because you are probably the kind of person who makes decisions on personal examination of the facts, rather than second-hand hearsay. A point comes in your research when you end up in the bookshop with this book in your hand. Give us five minutes of your undivided attention to read this first short chapter and you will be able to make that considered decision about online job hunting, in full possession of all the facts.

The Web might not be what you think. For many people, that tiresome 'Get online now' mantra can readily be translated into 'Spend £1,000 on a Web-ready computer so you can buy CDs without getting off the sofa.' Fortunately, the Web is much more than that.

Here are the facts: a survey performed by BMRB International of London found that online job hunting is the fourth most popular use of the Web in the UK after e-mail, shopping and booking travel. It is widely accepted that the vast majority of organizations are planning to increase Web recruitment efforts in the next year while decreasing traditional methods.

From large general job sites such as www.fish4jobs.com, www.workthing.com and www.monster.co.uk (which alone have over 400,000 job postings) to the 1,001 smaller sites that focus on every profession, level of expertise and region of the country, the Web has job opportunities for everyone. This book is your guide to the ocean of opportunities just awaiting the gentle click of your mouse.

> **job postings** Internet speak for a recruitment advertisement.

The benefits of an online job hunt rest on your computer's ability to create and change documents, and the incredible, unheard-of power of the World Wide Web for gathering and disseminating information:

- Creating information – creating CVs, covering letters, follow-up letters and the like. Without the Internet, you would ideally aim to customize your CV to each particular opportunity, but time would usually stand in the way, both for gathering the data needed and for the customizing itself. With Internet access, you can rapidly gather this information online, making the ensuing changes to a document like your CV with just a few clicks of the mouse.
- Gathering information – finding job openings and finding companies for which you would like to work. In the UK right now more than 3 million companies

have Web sites (www.domainstats.com), and those Web sites have company data you would spend weeks finding otherwise. Because of the time restraints you probably wouldn't invest the time and energy to find that information – but someone else would and that is likely to be your competition. Once you understand how the Web works, you can use search engines to help you sort through this information. Among the many other valuable skills you will learn while inside these covers is the ability efficiently to unearth just about any job available in the nation – or the world for that matter.

> **search engine** A super efficient personal assistant, who fetches anything you ask for in under a minute. This electronic kind of PA doesn't talk back either!

■ Disseminating information – getting employers' attention with your CV and covering letter. Normally this takes enormous amounts of time. You have to print the CVs and the letters, address the envelopes, lick the stamps and stuff the envelopes. It's time-consuming and frustrating, and leaves you with a nasty taste in your mouth. We can show you how to use an online job hunt to get your CV in front of thousands of employers in under an hour.

This online world can be difficult to grasp at first because anyone who understands it also seems to have an advanced degree in geek speak. They'll explain things to you for hours, and all you'll get is a pain in the neck. Not here. You don't need to be able to tell a bit from a byte, or to become a computer wizard. Driving a car is similar in that it can enhance your life but you don't need to know how the engine works. You just need to know where the petrol, oil, water and air go, how to steer, where the brake and accelerator are, and you're off into the wild blue yonder. This Web stuff is the same; you don't have to become a computer programmer to benefit from the invention.

When you use this book to implement an online job hunt, you will learn ways to conduct a more effective, faster and more comprehensive job hunt than you ever have before. Then when you are done and installed in your new job you'll find yourself in possession of new skills: you will be Internet-literate and able to apply what you have learnt in these pages to the day-to-day challenges of your professional work life. You will become better connected to your profession and your professional community, which will make future job changes much easier and smoother. You will learn how to manage and archive all the career-oriented information you gather, so that in the future you will have better control to implement your career management strategies.

Is there anything I really need to know about how this Web thing came about?

Nothing we can't breeze through in a couple of paragraphs. It all grew out of the cold war. In the 1960s the US Department of Defense wanted to create a communications network that would keep working even during a nuclear disaster. In the 1980s researchers, educators and the scientific community in Europe and the United States figured out they could use a form of this network to help them communicate their complex ideas and enormous amounts of data quickly and confidentially all over the globe. In the early 1990s word spread about the potential of this new communication medium and corporations like IBM and Netscape got involved and the rest, as they say, is history.

Without getting technical, the Web can deliver written and spoken word as well as live or recorded sound and pictures. This means that at your fingertips you can have magazine articles, books, radio, TV, one-to-one counselling and seminars all delivered to you on demand and to wherever you are sitting at the time you want to access the information. If you need to learn, gather and share information, as you do in a job hunt, there is simply no finer tool available.

Let's apply this to your online job hunt. As we show you how to run a highly effective online job hunt, we'll also show you where you can instantly:

- access electronic articles and books about job hunting;
- listen to experts talking about job-hunting techniques;
- watch experts discussing job-hunting techniques;
- get access to world-class career management authorities for one-to-one consultations;
- take live, interactive job-hunting courses with career experts.

Are the Web and the Internet the same thing?

If you want to impress your friends and family with some technical jargon ask them, 'What's the difference between the Internet and the World Wide Web?' They'll probably tell you they are the same thing. They are not. The Internet is a global association of computers that carries data and makes the exchange of information possible – it's the backbone that carries it all. The World Wide Web is just one type of data that the Internet communicates, mainly pictures and documents. Most of us access the Web only, because we want the documents, Web sites, e-mail and pictures that computers can read and show us. These are all called http documents – they are the ones that allow us to 'point' and 'click' on links to get from one Web site or document to another. Enough of the techno speak; let's get back to the business of job hunting.

> **http** Hyper Text Transfer Protocol – the set of rules and procedures that defines how messages are formatted, displayed and communicated over the Internet.

If the Web is this effective for online job hunting, everyone will be doing it, so how am I going to stand out?

As time goes by, more and more people will start to use online job-hunting techniques, but right now you are at the very forefront, and by being here you are going to get certain benefits. The world of work has changed dramatically over the last 10 years. Jobs that used to be mainstays have all but disappeared from the landscape of work, replaced by computers and machines. The essence of every remaining job has changed too. Many jobs have become much simpler (computers picking up much of that job's workload), with the result that they pay less and have no prospects for professional growth attached to them (referred to in the United States as McJobs after the famous burger chain). At the other end of the scale some jobs have become infinitely more complex. This has come about partly because of our shift into an information-based economy, and also because of the changing hierarchical structure of companies.

Companies are flatter with fewer levels of management and more responsibility devolving on to the individual worker's desk. One clear fact has emerged from this: companies are actively seeking computer- and Web-literate professionals, people who are maximally productive in managing themselves and their professional responsibilities.

So here is one of those hidden benefits to which you will become entitled as you read this book: when a company has an online recruitment initiative, they are ruling out the computer illiterate and screening in the technologically adapted. So when you apply for jobs online:

- You will have less competition because relatively few people are using this approach yet. The BMRB study we mentioned earlier also notes that a large percentage of people in the UK – nearly 30 per cent – have stated they have no intention of ever going online, so common sense tells you that you must be on to a good thing here.

- You will stand out by the very fact that you made your approach in this way. Effectively you are one of the early adapters, the first wave of Web users.
- The employer is expecting good things because of how you approached it. More time and attention will be paid to your CV.

Who can find a job on the Web?

You might think it is just the nerds that can benefit from an online aspect to their job hunt, but if so you would be very wrong. Already most companies are using their Web sites as recruiting portals for the company; and those that aren't today will be tomorrow, if for no other reason than that in today's world every company has to have a Web site, and once you have a Web site there is absolutely no reason not to use it as a recruitment tool.

Anyone can use the tricks we'll show you in this book to find a great new job – not just technical professionals. From new graduates to executives, full-time or part-time and from lorry drivers to doctors – anyone and everyone can use the Web to find that first or next step up the professional ladder. Remember that already over 3 million UK companies have Web sites. In fact, in Appendix A at the back of the book, we've put together a list of 1,001 job sites that cover more than 40 industries or professional categories.

Don't be afraid of the Web; all you need to do is understand the tools and the rules, and that's what this book will help you do. What you'll end up with is a new technological awareness and the means to manage your career better for the remainder of your work life. We won't bog you down with all the technical jargon but you will have a good handle on the essentials and will be able to implement this new knowledge immediately – and see results in terms of multiple interviews (more than you have ever had before) and job offers. We mean this. As you get into this book you will see that there is something practical and actionable on every page, something you can learn how to do and put to work for yourself right now today.

Do I have to have my own computer to use the Web in my job search?

No. But you will need the use of a computer with Web access – not necessarily your own at home, but a friend's, library or cybercafé computer will do.

Obviously having your own computer at home will make the whole process most comfortable. Who wouldn't like to surf the Web at midnight nibbling on popcorn with the dog at your feet? – but it's not mandatory. You don't need to spend a large sum of money to have the latest system, scanner, high-speed access and plasma monitor in your bedroom. Most libraries offer access, and Web cafés are springing up everywhere – why not get a vanilla double latte, a date and a new job all at one time? However, if you will be using a friend's or a publicly accessed computer, pay careful attention to our advice on organization and privacy in the following chapters.

OK, I'm buying this so far, but let's get specific here: how am I going to use the Web to find jobs?

With electronic databases you'll be able to get your CV in front of thousands of employers and recruiters in a couple of hours, and you'll be able to locate hundreds of jobs in the same time-frame. This ease and firepower would be impossible under traditional methods of research and distribution.

> **electronic databases** Think of reference books where instead of having to read everything you simply say what it is you want and the book automatically turns to the right page.

Traditional recruitment advertising is rapidly moving online. The online equivalent of the help wanted section of the newspaper is the job bank. Today in the UK there are over 1 million jobs posted on the top 10 job banks alone, and that number is growing daily. It would take you weeks and months to find these by reading newspapers and magazines; online you can do it in a fraction of the time.

A job bank lists the jobs just like your newspaper does. The big difference is that you don't have to go blind-reading through them all; the computer will do that for you. We'll explain how the job banks and search engines work, and show you what they look like and how to type in a few keywords that will enable your computer to come up with the jobs that match your criteria. And we'll connect you with 1,001 job sites of all types from the gargantuan general job boards to the highly specialized sites. By the way, once you have told a job bank what you are looking for, many have the ability to contact you whenever a matching job gets posted. So you don't have to go back every week to see if there are any new openings.

The Web also allows the employer or headhunter to find you in ways that never existed before. Just as there are job banks, there are also CV banks. In fact, most job banks also have a CV bank on site. Anyone can post his or her electronic CV on a CV bank (and yes, we'll show you how to build an outstanding electronic CV). There are already hundreds of these CV banks, some with 5,000 CVs posted and some with upwards of 500,000 posted. A CV bank is a useful tool because you can anonymously post your credentials for viewing by interested parties. Now because companies want to hire Web-literate professionals, human resource departments and executive recruiters are actively searching these CV banks on a daily basis.

OK, but what else can I do? There are some specific international conglomerates I'd like to work for. Can I find local positions with them?

You can use the Web to find specific types of companies or local locations of a particular company for which you have always wanted to work. There are tools available to help you identify companies within your industry – companies you may have never known existed. Likewise, we'll teach you a few tricks on how to find a specific company's Web site and how to find job and contact information once you're there.

The Web is growing like a boom town, and that means the buildings and infrastructure are under constant construction, so don't expect seamless perfection. Yet with all the problems you might expect, the benefits far outweigh the drawbacks.

Business and industry have already adopted the Web as an effective recruitment medium and it's growing at an unbelievable rate because it's cost-effective, time-efficient and allows the employer to identify talent that is up to date with the latest technologies and business communication techniques.

Why should I believe that there will be a job for me on the Web?

The five top reasons are:

1. Company Web sites host many jobs – over 1 million per year.
2. Businesses post tens of thousands of jobs each day to online job banks.
3. Employers now have staff and budgets specifically earmarked for online recruitment.

4. The majority of employers and recruiters have implemented online methods and tools in their recruitment process.
5. Online job searching is not only for technical professionals – non-technical job postings and CVs now outnumber technical ones.

What do I need to do to get started using the Web in my job search?

Here's a quick overview of what you need to conduct an effective online job hunt, and how this book will help you.

Yes, you will still need a CV and it will need to be a little different from the ones you have created in the past. Don't despair; what we'll show you isn't hard to grasp and will be easy to implement, and there are some really useful ways you can exploit the process. Your CV is the primary tool an employer needs to evaluate your eligibility for an interview but its creation process has some real benefits to you too.

In creating your CV you will package yourself as a saleable professional commodity. Done properly, it will open doors and get employers excited about the prospect of meeting you. Not only that, most interviewers use your CV as their roadmap for the interview, so in its creation you are helping guide the path your live interviews will take. And finally, long after the last interview is over, the hiring manager will use your CV as part of the final review process for who gets hired over whom.

An electronic CV is different from a paper version. For instance, there are two or three formats that might be suitable for your online job hunt. You will learn what they are and we will show you how to build them without confusing you with science, and using only the bare minimum of computer jargon.

You will also need to create covering letters and the like; they vary somewhat from the traditional kind, so we'll make sure you get a good grasp on what works and why, and what doesn't and how to avoid those pitfalls. You will also learn how to get them into Web-compatible formats.

Any job hunt should be conducted in a way that protects your professional integrity. We'll show you how to set up specific (and free) e-mail accounts for your job hunt. This will simplify handling the large number of leads you will quickly amass, just as it protects your confidentiality. After all, you don't want just anyone knowing that you are moving on, moving up and moving out – at least, not yet.

Your current job hunt is unlike any other you have done before (times have changed) and you undoubtedly have unique circumstances in your life that will affect the exact strategy you will use. The authors have over 40 years in the career management and job-hunting business and we also have 14 years' online experience between us in these very same areas. You won't find anyone in the world with better credentials. We are on top of this as seasoned career management professionals, and we'll do our best to help you succeed.

We will also discuss strategies to help you put the power of the Web to your best advantage. You'll need to assess your personal situation and decide what type of job hunt you need to implement. For example, the full-scale attack (see below) would not be a good approach for someone currently employed or for a senior-level executive. Your assessment will help you apply the knowledge in the book to a plan that fits your unique needs. Those needs are likely to fit into one of these four essential categories:

- Full-scale attack – you might be unemployed or newly graduated, or need a job immediately, and have no reason for top-level confidentiality. You want to pull out all the stops, get maximum response and get back to work, or out to work as soon as possible.
- Mini attack – a more focused version of the full-scale attack. You might use select job boards, specialist sites, associations and specific company site research. The target attack can be confidential or not and can also be ideal for someone who has identified a couple of poten-

tial career paths or is interested in a full career or industry change. This is ideal if you are still employed but have informed your employer (or vice versa) that you are looking for a change.

- Secret attack – the strategy for someone who is employed and needs a totally confidential approach, or for someone who just wants to keep an eye on the scene (good career management). It is better to know and reject available opportunities rather than slave in that high-rise salt mine never knowing your options. Typically only confidential CVs are posted, and sites are used that deliver jobs to you rather than involve you in going to search for the jobs.
- Mission *not* impossible attack – when you know the exact company or companies that you want to work for. Essentially it is finding a way to get in the door via research, company executive profiles, association members and the like. This is how you get deep inside your industry and make the mission impossible very possible.

Whichever of these approaches is right for your situation, these pages will show you how to implement an effective plan of attack, as we give you great answers to all your tough online job-hunting questions. If you really heed what we say in the coming pages you can ensure that your next step is a step up.

two

What kind of CV do I need online?

When I do my online job hunt, will I still need to write and mail my CV?

Yes. But there are a few changes to be aware of – not afraid of, just aware of. This is a book about online job hunting, not a book on CV writing from the ground up. In the next few pages, however, we are going to show you how to beef up your existing CV and make it a more powerful marketing tool, whether you use it online or offline.

We are going to focus on some key elements of your professional work history and skill sets that will help your CV stand out in whatever medium you use to distribute it. This chapter will walk you through these steps, and then show you how to develop your CV into a format suitable for online distribution.

Let's start at the beginning. Your CV is still your calling card. Whether an employer is looking for a candidate online or offline, your CV will be your ticket to landing the interview. Prospective employers are looking for a new employee because they have a problem to solve. You can look at any job opening, at any level, and in any profession this way: problems to solve equal job opening; no problems to solve equal no job opening. When it comes down to it, anyone ever hired for any job is hired to be a problem solver. This is a good concept to keep in mind as you build your CV. What challenges and problems are you paid to solve in your professional life? It is a good idea to use your CV to show that you are a problem solver.

As you key in your CV, it will help you identify your professional strengths and selling points. Identifying these areas is one of the most important steps you go through in a job hunt, because these are the very types of illustrations you will use in your answers to the employers' tough interview questions.

So how do you figure out the accomplishments and abilities you bring to the table?

Here's an easy exercise that will help you see yourself more clearly – let's face it, it can be hard to take credit for the things you do every single day of your working life. You are usually too busy chopping down trees to step back and see the size of the clearing you have made in the forest. To give yourself some perspective try this:

1. Write down your most recent or current position title. Next to it, write down any other titles you have heard that describe the same job.
2. Write a few sentences describing each of your daily duties, functions and responsibilities. Take some time on this; really think about what you do on a daily, weekly and annual basis. What areas of the company do you affect?
3. Think of these activities in terms of the problems they solve for the company. Difficult? Think of the problems that would exist if you weren't there to solve or stop them from occurring in the first place.
4. Once you've done that, analyse and list what skills you need in order to perform those duties effectively.

5. Finally, prove that you have performed those duties effectively. You do this by citing specific achievements and facts – stories, if you will, that demonstrate what you've done and how well you've done it.

Here is an example of what your exercise might look like:

Title: Purchasing Manager.

Duty: negotiate large purchases while maintaining stock turnover standards.

Problems: source best-quality, most reliable and competitively priced material and supplies so we as a company can compete most effectively in our marketplace.

Skills: formal training; knowledge of product shelf-life and sales cycle; deep understanding of purchasing processes and payment options; strong communication and negotiating skills.

Achievements: reduced product purchasing cost by 5 per cent and finance charges by 2.5 per cent; increased profit by £180,000.

Important note: if you can assign monetary values, actual numbers or percentages to these claims, they will make impressive additions to your CV and substantiate your claims.

The best way to demonstrate your ability to solve an employer's problem is to tell the employer what you have achieved in the past – those things that set you apart from your competition. If you saved the company money, make a conservative estimate as to how much. If you saved them time (which also means money), estimate how much. Now, be careful not to overestimate or exaggerate to make yourself look good; however, don't forget to take credit for the accomplishments of a team you were a member of as well. This can make your claim more believable and it will demonstrate your ability to work with others.

Achievements will vary depending on your function and level of responsibility. Those in sales can easily quantify accomplishments as sales quota or new customer acquisition. Technical and production professionals tend to quantify their accomplishments based on increased productivity, which equates to money and profitability. Administrative professionals might use time and labour reductions as cost savings accomplishments. Executives will look at the big picture and use overall revenues and profitability as a measure of success.

Getting a handle on your achievements is too important for us to chance that you don't quite have a handle on it. So, if you are struggling with this concept, try this exercise as well:

1. Imagine you are meeting with your supervisor to discuss your rise or a bonus. Quickly, without a lot of concentration, write down everything you can think of to win that cash. Fill in the details later but picture specific instances where you made a difference – that's why you deserve the money.
2. Next, think of and write down your two toughest job-related challenges. Go back over your last couple of jobs if you have to.
3. Describe how you resolved the problem, step by step, by yourself or as a member of a team.
4. Consider the professional skills and behaviours you employed to achieve this: analytical, time management skills, determination, etc. When you talk about your skills and behaviours in a CV or during an interview, you are describing a conscientious professional. For more on the identification and integration of desirable professional behaviours, see the companion volume, *Great Answers to Tough Interview Questions* (published by Kogan Page).
5. Finally, quantify your result. Your solution saved your employer money, time or both, or earned money. Take an educated guess.

Don't skip these exercises – including accomplishments and

problem-solving abilities in your CV will make a dramatic impact in your job-search success.

So, what style CV is best for an online job hunt?

You've probably heard of three basic CV styles: the chronological, the functional and the combination. A chronological CV is one that lists the employment history in reverse order, with details provided for each position. A functional CV emphasizes the relevant skills and accomplishments of the writer without focusing on order of the positions held – best for someone with a sketchy work history or a job hopper. A combination CV, just as it sounds, offers a bit of both – a section of skills and accomplishments and a reverse work history. By far the most popular styles (both online and offline) are combination and chronological, but a powerful chronological CV will have heavy emphasis on accomplishments and problem-solving abilities. Our examples in this chapter will be based on combination and chronological CVs.

If you are unsure of the style of CV best suited to you, find a CV book dedicated to the topic, or professional CV-writing advice. Professional CV writers and career coaches are abundant, and the links we provide in Appendix A will guide you to many. Just as a mechanic can fix the strange rattle in your car engine, so a certified career professional can be of great assistance to anyone who has had trouble maintaining employment or is changing career fields entirely.

A CV works most powerfully on your behalf when it demonstrates what you have done for past employers and therefore what you will do for the next company lucky enough to get you. Let's take this CV to the next level – the electronic level. What does that mean? Primarily three things:

- It has to have keywords.
- It must be scannable.
- It must be capable of communication not only on paper but also over the Web through e-mail – and in multiple formats.

So what is this new CV technology that recruiters and companies are using? And what do I have to do to make my CV electronically effective?

To make your CV effective, you need to put yourself into the shoes of the people who will be reviewing it and understand what processes they use. The vast majority of human resource professionals and managers are using new online resources, technology and software to speed up and improve the recruiting process. The better you understand the process, the more likely you are to get your CV read by real human eyes.

Increasingly, companies are storing the CVs they receive in electronic databases, regardless of whether or not you send an electronic or a paper CV. This gives you a new challenge in getting your CV read by human eyes, so it is fortunate that we can show you how to make that happen.

It all started a few years ago when two software programs hit the market: Resumix and Restrac. In the beginning only large companies could afford these programs, which essentially allowed the company to scan or digitally input CVs and then save them to be accessed later using keyword and other criteria. But competition and the Internet made scanning and searching CVs available to virtually any size of company or recruiter.

If you send an electronic CV it will automatically be stored in such a database. If you send a traditional paper CV, the chance increases every day that it too will end up in an electronic database, having first been run through a scanner to digitize it.

Once in the database it is lost to human sight, and whether or not it ever again sees the light of day depends entirely on how well you apply what we are going to share with you in the next couple of pages. To get your CV picked by the computer really isn't that difficult once you understand how the software that reads the database works to sort one CV from another.

Here's the simple truth: virtually any HR professional can sit in an office and access a database of hundreds of thousands of CVs by typing in a few select words. So you must have a CV that will be accepted into a CV database, and one that contains enough of the right keywords so that it will get pulled out again for human review.

In today's electronic world, you not only need a paper CV that is scannable, but you also need an electronic CV – specifically a text-based e-mail CV. Now, we just threw a bunch of jargon at you, but relax if you don't understand these terms; we will tackle each one on its own as well as what to do. Let's talk for a moment about keywords.

What are keywords, why do I need them and where do I put them in my CV?

With the advent of CV software and electronic databases, when an employer needs to sort through CVs for likely job candidates, he or she just goes to the keyboard, types in a job title and is presented with a list of descriptors: words that describe different aspects of that job. Keywords can be nouns or verbs as well as two- or three-word catchphrases, depending on the industry or function. Some of these words will be verbs such as:

- design;
- implement;
- plan;
- sell;
- manage;

- review;
- control;
- conceive.

And some will be nouns, often in combination with other nouns, like:

- information technology;
- market share;
- business development;
- public relations;
- product development.

As job responsibilities with the same title differ from company to company, the software has extensive lists of keywords for every conceivable job title. The user will click on those words that most closely describe the specific job to be filled.

For example, a public relations firm might be looking for an experienced account executive who can bring in new business and develop effective campaigns from start to finish. As the recruiter scrolls down the list of keyword options, he or she will click on 'public relations', 'new business' and probably 'conceive', 'design' and 'implement' too, because the company needs someone who can solve its problem, finding someone who can: bring in new business; and conceive, design and implement effective PR campaigns.

The recruiter will continue to click on keywords as they seem relevant descriptors for the job to be filled. Once the recruiter has finished clicking, the software program will search the database for documents (ie CVs) that contain any of these keywords. It will then rank the documents it finds according to the number and frequency of the keywords found, the CV with the most matches being ranked number one, and so on down the list.

Now CV reading is very demanding, so this tool is a godsend to the corporate recruiter. The problem for you though is that you have to design your CV with this requirement in mind.

To help you with this, we have created an extensive keyword database at the back of this book in Appendix B. This keyword list includes action verbs that apply to all jobs, and profession-specific descriptor nouns. We don't intend you to make up a CV that uses the words at the expense of accurately describing your capabilities. We do however expect you to review the words and see how they or more relevant descriptors of your own could be included in your CV.

How do you determine what keywords are right for you?

When you did the exercise at the beginning of this chapter to help you uncover your problem-solving skills, you probably noticed some repetition when describing your duties and skills. One great way to find keywords offline for your profession is to look through recent newspaper ads. After you've found 10 to 15 adverts you are interested in, start listing words and phrases common to the group. Many of those same words are probably in your CV – if not, they should be.

How can I make sure I have enough keywords in my CV?

Each CV is different and much of that depends on the amount of experience you have. To help illustrate different and effective methods of increasing the number of keywords in a CV, we offer three examples in the following pages. Each of the job seekers in these examples has a differing background and amount of experience. Let's take a look at each one and the various methods and areas where we can include additional keywords.

First, let's look at a typical professional with about 10 years' experience (see Figure 2.1).

Under our fictitious Mr Brown's Professional Profile lead-in, there is a Skill Set section. This is an easy, professional way to include extra keywords in your CV. It tells the reader that here are a number of areas, perhaps not all addressed in the CV, where you have problem-solving skills and accomplishments. So it acts as a teaser, as an encouragement to get into direct conversation with you, and that after all is the goal of any CV.

Now, if you are a new graduate or someone who lacks a great deal of experience, we have another suggestion. Figure 2.2 is the CV of a new graduate, Miss Holmes with an education in accountancy. As the necessary keywords may not be considered developed skills at this point, we suggest listing several relevant course titles as well as a skills section.

And to show you that even executives will benefit from keywords, although they may not think that a keyword section is professional, the example (Figure 2.3) shows that using an alternative heading, summary and additional accomplishments statements can achieve the same goal. Mr

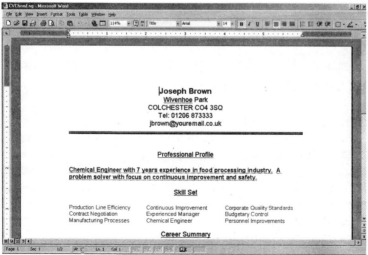

Figure 2.1 Joseph Brown's CV

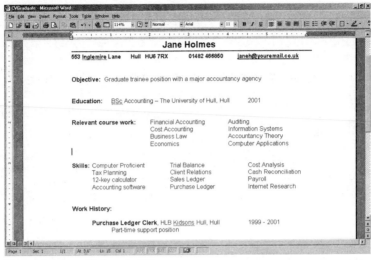

Figure 2.2 Jane Holmes's CV

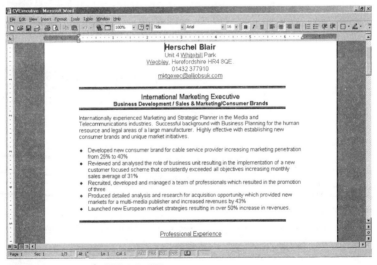

Figure 2.3 Herschel Blair's CV

Blair has craftily incorporated keywords into his heading, executive summary and list of primary achievements.

What is a scannable CV and why do I need one?

We spoke earlier about companies using the latest technology to build databases of CVs that they can search at their convenience. In order to do that, the CVs must be entered into the computer system. Electronically delivered CVs enter the database automatically, but the ones you send by mail must first be scanned and digitized, so your CV has to be scanner-friendly. Obviously no one wants to sit there and type in hundreds of documents, so that's where this scanning technology comes into play.

> **scanning** The process used to take a hard copy or fax document (your CV) and convert it to a digital document within a computer database.

This is what happens. A company receives your paper CV and they place it in a scanner that takes a picture of your CV. Then they apply a software program called OCR (optical character recognition) to that picture. The OCR software tries to identify parts of that picture that represent letters, numbers and symbols. The idea is that in the end, the picture of your CV becomes a series of words and numbers that can be searched through by the employer – and no one had to type it in (except you in the beginning).

A scannable CV relies on the ability of the company's OCR software. So, be proactive – make your CV as scannable as possible. Here are some things to be careful of when creating a scannable CV:

- Always avoid paper with too much colour, a coloured border, a heavy watermark or graining – plain white paper is best.

■ Never print a border around a document or around a section of text in the CV. The OCR software could identify the outline as a single character and omit the contents of that section (see Figure 2.4).

■ Do not use columns – the order of the words would be out of sequence and that could hurt the effectiveness of your keyword sections.

■ Do not use font smaller than 10 point. Although scanner and OCR software is always improving, you are not sure of the individual capabilities of any employer or recruiter – so don't chance it.

■ Likewise, many experts are on the fence as to the scanning ability of italics, bold, underline, etc. Older versions of OCR software had problems with embellishments like these, which the newer versions are better able to handle. So in reality some companies that receive your CV will scan it accurately with all your bold, italics, underlines and the like. Older programs on the other hand will mess up your CV as a result. So we recommend you spend more time on the keywords and keep the layout simple and embellishments to a minimum.

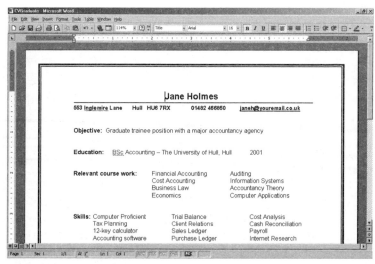

Figure 2.4 A border in a CV

When should I use a scannable CV?

In today's world, whenever you send or fax a hard copy CV to a company, assume that it will be scanned. Whether you know it or not, whether the company asked for a scannable CV or not, there is an ever increasing possibility that it will be scanned. Most companies do it, so it's best to assume it will be scanned; this way you will design it accordingly. You simply have too much to lose – if you don't send a scannable CV, the chances are that the company will file your CV in the circular file and you will never have a chance at the job.

By the way, when faxing be sure to use 'fine mode' to ensure better resolution. When we speak of faxing, we typically speak of faxing a paper copy from one fax machine to another. This is a new computer age so it is worth mentioning that you can fax from you desktop – directly from your computer. Most new PCs come with standard software that allows you to fax a document or receive one without having to print it.

OK, I have my problem-solving, keyword-packed, scannable paper CV – now how do I turn it into an electronic CV?

Don't get scared now! You've done all the hard work writing and building a dynamic CV full of powerful stories about you and packed with keywords to get you to the top of the employer's database search. So, the only thing left is to make it digital. Let's remove all concepts of a paper CV and take this scanning thing out of our minds completely.

An electronic CV is one built on a computer, e-mailed via the Web and on receipt usually downloaded into an employer's electronic CV database. There are three different ways you can distribute your CV electronically: ASCII or plain text; formatted text; and Web-based/HTML.

You may not need all of them, but you will need at least the first two, if not all three. Here is a description of all three types:

▪ Plain text or ASCII is the simplest version. We're talking just the basics, only text, letters, numbers and a few symbols found on your keyboard. ASCII (American Standard Code for Information Exchange) CVs are important because this is the only format that any computer type (PC or Mac) can read. No word processor is necessary (Microsoft Word or WordPerfect), and there is no software or printer compatibility to consider, just the plain, cold hard text:
  – no fancy formatting;
  – no bolded words;
  – no bullets;
  – no italics;
  – nothing underlined;
  – nothing made 'pretty'.
An ASCII CV looks like a plain old text e-mail message. It's not an attachment. Your CV is directly in the body of the e-mail message. We will get on to creating this version in just a few more paragraphs.

▪ A formatted electronic CV is a CV that is also sent via e-mail, but as an attachment. Using your word processor (like Microsoft Word or WordPerfect), you send a 'pretty' CV with all the formatting, bullets, bolding, underlines, etc. But you do so in a manner that allows the employer to download it directly into a CV software package. So, two things are important:
  – You must be using a compatible word-processing program. You cannot send the employer a CV in Word if the only program the employer has is Word Perfect. These compatibility issues are becoming fewer and fewer as programs come with converting packages, but at the present time the elegance of your formatted CV could still get lost in the conversion. Remember Murphy's Law: whatever can go wrong will go wrong.

- As the formatted electronic CV is still being down-loaded into a CV software package, you must be sure to include appropriate keywords.

When responding to an employer that has not indicated a preferred word-processing format, the safest bet is to include an ASCII CV in the e-mail body as well as the formatted attachment. We will explain everything you need to know about creating and sending your CV as an attachment in Chapter 4.

A Web CV is not a 'must have' for everyone. Essentially, a Web CV (or Web portfolio) is an electronic formatted CV that is housed on the Internet. A Web CV has a few advantages in that you will typically take advantage of multimedia including audio and video clips, music and pictures. Who should have a Web CV? Well, if you are in a creative profession and would typically have a port-folio, then a Web CV can allow access to your work samples. In today's Internet-friendly world, showing your creative and electronic abilities could attract the right employer.

The primary goal of any CV is to get you into conversation with employers; you want to be specific enough to get their attention, yet vague enough for them to have to get into conversation with you to learn more. The danger with a Web-based CV is that it can reveal so much about you that an employer can make a decision without speaking to you – not good.

In creating a Web-based CV, you end up building a multi-media Web site that features pictures, and streamed audio and video. It takes time to learn an entirely new set of skills. We don't recommend you invest the time in your first online job hunt; instead, we suggest you focus on the two text-based formats.

However, if you have the time, talent and energy, go ahead. Don't go crazy, and keep it professional. You don't want a Web CV with pictures of your family, hobbies or pets. Be sure to password-protect your Web CV or portfolio. You want to control who sees what you have to offer.

So, how do I make my CV an ASCII CV?

Converting your keyword-packed CV into a text or ASCII version is not difficult. There are two easy ways to do this; we'll explain both of them and you can decide which is easier for you. The end result is the same, so it's a matter of personal preference.

First, open your CV in whatever word-processing program you use. The most popular in today's world is Microsoft Word, so that's what we'll use in our example. Let's use our new graduate's CV (see Figure 2.5).

Assuming you have spell-checked and perfected your CV, open it in your word processor, make a duplicate copy and save the duplicate under a new name, let's say ELEC-TRONIC RESUME -1. Now you are ready to try either or both of the conversion methods.

Method 1 is:

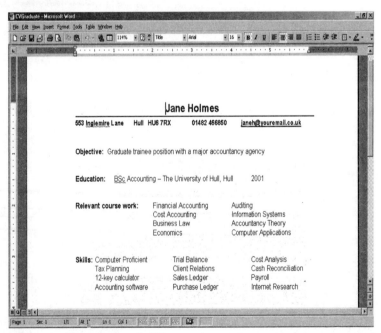

Figure 2.5 New graduate's CV

1. Copy the entire document by choosing 'Select All' from the 'Edit' pull-down menu (Cmd+A for Macintosh) and then choosing 'Copy' from the 'Edit' pull-down menu or Ctrl+C for Windows (Cmd+C for Macintosh) (see Figure 2.6).

2. Open a new document in your word processor. Set margins to 60 characters per line, which equates to margins of about 1.7 to 1.75 inches on both the left and right sides (see Figure 2.7). You could count out 60 characters if that's easier for you. The reason you need to limit the number of characters in each line is because the majority of electronic screens are limited to that viewing width so you do not want text to 'wrap off the screen'.

3. Next you are going to 'Paste' the CV you just copied into this new document. To do that, simply choose 'Paste' from the 'Edit' pull-down menu or Ctrl+V for Windows (or Cmd+V for Macintosh). Initially, the document will look very similar to your previous CV, but we will be modifying in more.

4. Once again, go to the 'Edit' pull-down menu and choose 'Select All' (Cmd+A for Macintosh). Now you are going

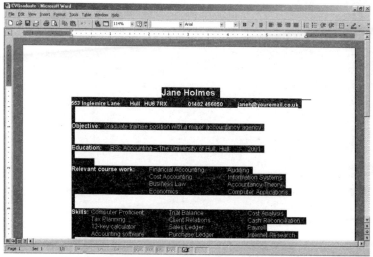

Figure 2.6 Copying the CV

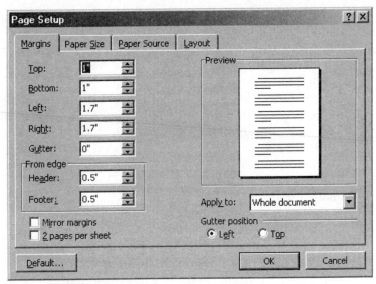

Figure 2.7 Setting the margins

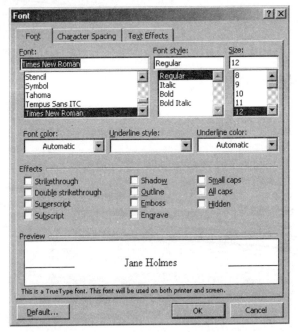

Figure 2.8 Setting the font

to change the font type and size. To do this choose 'Font' from the 'Format' pull-down menu and change the font type to Times New Roman or Courier and the size to 12 point (see Figure 2.8).

5. Now you will start to notice the CV changing, but we're still not done. We need to save this new document using the 'Save As' command but select the document type as 'Text Only' and rename. Let's call it Text Resume 1 (see Figure 2.9). When you do this, you will get a message box telling you that you will lose your formatting and asking you if you want to continue. You'll need to answer 'yes' because you do need to lose the formatting; that's what an ASCII or text-based CV is all about.

6. You will notice the document has lost many of its features and 'pretty looks', and that the spacing has gone awry (see Figure 2.10).

7. Now you will need to go over this new document very carefully to flush it to the left by removing empty spaces and tabs. You will need to use 'All caps' for section headers, and to replace text that was bolded or underlined. Likewise, all of your bullets are gone, and you

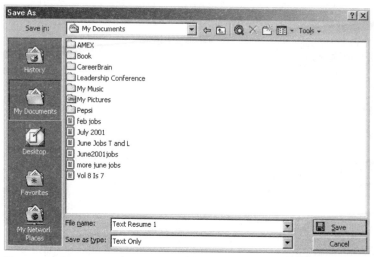

Figure 2.9 Saving in 'Text Only' format

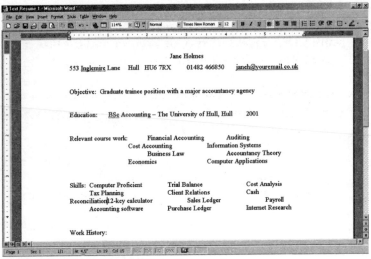

Figure 2.10 Text document when first saved

will either have to adjust the spacing to create an emphasis or use characters on your keyboard such as * and =. Once properly edited, our new graduate's CV looks like the one in Figure 2.11, and we will once again save the document to protect all the changes we have made. And remember, spell-check, edit and edit...

Method 2 is:

1. This method accomplishes the same end result but utilizes a text-based word processor such as WordPad or Notepad. Every type of computer has one, and it is typically found under the 'Accessories' section group.

2. Once in WordPad or Notepad, create a new document and make sure the 'Word Wrap' function is 'on'. To do this go to the 'Edit' pull-down menu and make sure there is a checkmark next to the menu choice 'Word Wrap'. If there is not, select it. This saves you having to set margins or count characters. That is one advantage of using a simple text-based program such as WordPad or Notepad.

3. Just as in the previous method, 'Copy' your CV from

your word processor and then 'Paste' it into the new WordPad or Notepad document (see Figure 2.12). (See Method 1, steps 1 and 3. All the steps are the same except you will paste into the WordPad or Notepad

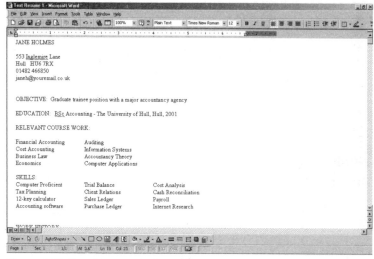

Figure 2.11 Text document after editing

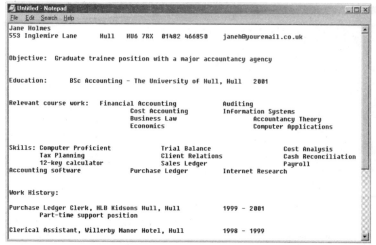

Figure 2.12 Copying and pasting into Notepad

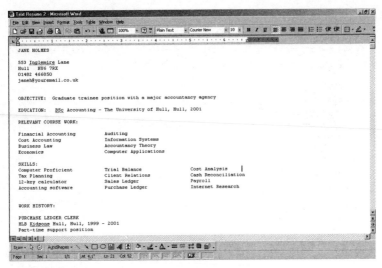

Figure 2.13 The notepad document after editing

document instead of your other word-processing program.)

4. Just as in the previous method, you will need to edit for spacing and use 'All caps' to add effectiveness (see Figure 2.13). The one step you do not have to do is to change the size or type of the font because, in the simple WordPad or Notepad program, the default settings are exactly what we need to create our ASCII text-based CV.

5. Once we've made our edits, checked our spelling and looked at our spacing options, let's save our work (see Figure 2.14).

So, there you have it – your text-based, keyword-packed ACSII CV ready to go!

This doesn't seem too difficult; what's next?

You will distribute your CV to a couple of types of destination. You will load it into CV banks where it will stand on its

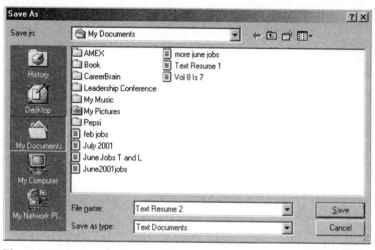

Figure 2.14 Saving the Notepad document

own keywords. You will also send to specific people via e-mail. In this second instance, although the CV will still ultimately end up in an electronic database, there is the chance that it can get a careful perusal first.

Your very best chances of setting up fast interviews occur when human eyes evaluate your e-CV before it goes into the databank. Getting that e-CV read with something approaching serious attention is what the next chapter is all about.

> **e-CV** Shorthand for an electronic CV.

three

What do I do about Internet covering letters?

Do I still need covering letters in my online job hunt?

The electronic recruitment process has become both a boon and a bane to recruiters using it. On the one hand, electronic recruitment can be more efficient; at the same time it yields a wider array of qualified candidates. On the other hand, the response rate can be overwhelming in volume. Hence the dramatic growth of CV banks, and CV software that scans the CV banks by keywords.

A great CV is one thing but, however it is delivered, you still need to make sure it is read with something approaching serious attention. A powerful covering letter can help you to make it stand out from the crowd. Now while this is always the case with a traditionally sent CV, things are not so clearly cut and dried with electronic distribution.

Sometimes your e-mail covering letter and CV will be opened by a real human being, read and acted upon. Sometimes your entire e-mail (CV and covering letter) will be automatically loaded directly into a CV bank, only to be read when it is subsequently pulled out because of its keyword content. In other instances you will be asked not to send a covering letter at all. And finally your CV and covering letter may meet a low-level functionary on the receiving end. This person's job may be to separate the letter and CV into separate documents or to load only the CV itself into the data bank.

So you can see that with online CV distribution the issues are more complex. How do you deal with this? While there is no absolute guarantee when or if your covering letter will get read, for the times that it will you are strongly advised to take the time to make it a candidacy-enhancing tool.

Today, most communications, especially e-mails, are getting shorter. Get to the point or you will lose the reader's attention. We have spoken to executives who will delete an e-mail message if the subject line (which we will get to in Chapter 4) and first two sentences do not tell them the purpose of the message – and give them a reason to supply their time and attention. Your covering letter is aimed at this very audience.

It used to be that your covering letter was the appetizer that got the juices going for the main course – your CV. In today's 'Give it to me fast and give it to me straight' world of e-mail communications, a covering letter has to get to the point in a hurry. This means keeping it short, while paying attention to keywords and conveying the purpose of the e-mail – why someone should read your CV – by quickly stating the facts: who you are, why you are writing and what makes you so qualified.

Hard copy covering letters tend to consist of three to five carefully constructed paragraphs (never longer than one page). They strategically emphasize this point and that point and maybe a few items that the CV just couldn't get across. The electronic covering letter is typically limited to two to five sentences and one screen length. Think of your e-mail messages. A screen length is the amount of a message you can read without having to scroll down the message. That typically means one paragraph.

Let's focus on the content of these letters. We've established the fact that our electronic covering letters need to be short. Our task is to tell the reader quickly why we are sending this message and give him or her a reason to read our CV. Here are some samples; look for the ways in which the letters build a bridge between the writer and the reader, uses keywords, makes a point about suitability and then asks for the next step:

I was excited to see your opening for a Bookkeeper vacancy on the accountingweb.co.uk Web site, Job 71601. As my CV below shows, this is a perfect match for my background in payroll, general ledger and accounts receivable. I welcome the opportunity to discuss my skills and your job requirements in greater detail.

While browsing the jobs database on Clickajob.com, I was intrigued by your Regional Sales Manager job posting. Although I am currently employed by one of your competitors, I have kept my eye open for an opportunity to join your organization. I believe my ability to build a sales force, attract new accounts and manage a new product introduction will intrigue you as well. Please review my CV below and contact me confidentially to schedule a time for us to meet.

It was great meeting you for lunch the other day. As you suggested I have attached a copy of my current CV. Since our meeting I have given more thought to your company goals and believe they are closely related to my skills and career goals. If I don't hear from you this week, I'll call you next week to schedule a time when we can continue our conversation.

Your colleague, Jon Ferguson, suggested that I send you my CV. Jon mentioned that your department is looking for Electrical Engineers with experience in product development and sterile environments. As my CV below demonstrates, that is precisely the work I have done for six years. I welcome the opportunity to discuss your specific projects and explore the possibility of joining your team.

Although I am currently employed by one of your major competitors, I became enthralled while browsing your company Web site. I found your company philosophy and growth plans to be of significant interest to me. Your dedication to continual process improvement and latest technology implementation aroused my interest, because these are precisely my areas of expertise – as my CV below indicates. With significant experience in areas of importance to your firm, I look forward to the opportunity to discuss available opportunities.

My colleague Rebecca Howard recommended your recruiting firm to me, as you assisted her successfully to join Last Chance Finance as a Business Development Director. I understand that your firm specializes in the consumer products industry with particular attention to sales, marketing and business development vacancies. As a current Marketing Director with 12 years of experience in consumer products, I am hoping that my CV attached will be of interest. Please call me at my home number to discuss any openings for which your firm is conducting searches.

Each of these sample electronic covering letters follows a similar format. Each does three things: identifies how it came to be that you are sending your CV; states why the reader should read the CV; and asks for the interview or next contact. Let's take a closer look at each of these elements:

1. Identify what made you make contact. Whether it was through a job posting, a colleague, finding them on the Internet or that they are a recruiting firm, tell the reader you see a match. If it is a job posting, indicate the job title and job number if there is one (often job boards will have jobs listed by number – more about this in Chapter 5). Likewise, if a friend or colleague is involved, state that person's name and connection. If you found them while conducting research or through networking, state that as well.
2. Give the reader a reason to read your CV. This is also

where you can stick in keywords. State the link, what the job posting indicated the company is looking for or why your friend saw a possible connection; talk about your experience and skill sets. If there is a chance to whet the reader's appetite, this is the place. Likewise, if you are currently employed or work for a competitor – say it! This not only provides you with confidentiality, but many companies seek the expertise from competitors and thrive on luring such expertise away.

3. Ask for the next step. Suggest a meeting, phone call or interview. Indicate that you will be following up the contact if it's appropriate. Don't be afraid to ask.

Now that we've spoken about the rules of electronic covering letters and discussed a content strategy, we need to write samples and get them into an electronic format – just like we did with the CV in the last chapter. So, let's get started. We suggest you do this, not in your e-mail program but with your standard word-processing program. This way you can save each different letter you write as a template for future needs. It is certain that if you have a need for a particular type of covering letter once, you will have the need again.

Am I going to need more than one covering letter?

Absolutely. You have to consider the audience to whom the letters are going. Typically you will be sending your CV and covering letter:

- in response to online job postings;
- to friends and professional colleagues;
- to companies and contacts you've found from reference works, newspapers, trade publications and the Internet;
- to recruiters and headhunters.

Each of these letters, to each of these people, will require a customized and slightly different covering letter. The key to saving yourself time and being able to respond quickly in this electronic world is to develop templates from which to work.

Step 1

Open your word processor. (We will again use Microsoft Word because of its popularity.) Create a new document.

Unlike regular business letters, e-mail letters do not follow typical letter-writing protocols. For example, you would not put the date – the e-mail message is automatically dated. Likewise, it is not necessary to put the recipient's postal address or for that matter company name and title. The proper way to start a business e-mail message is with a simple salutation followed by the person's name. Do not address the sender by first name, as this can seem overly familiar.

If we were to use one of our sample covering letters, it would look like the example in Figure 3.1.

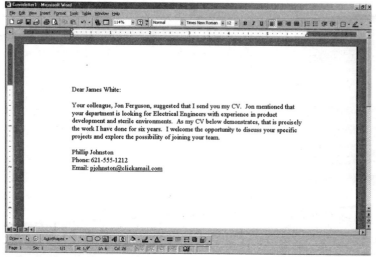

Figure 3.1 Sample covering letter

You will notice that the letter is signed by the sender's name, followed by telephone number and e-mail address. This is one instance when electronic mail and traditional job-hunting mail still abide by the same rules. In this instance the rule is that every page of every document you send should include your contact information. Just as with our CV, you need to spell-check your covering letter at this point and save the file. Let's call this one coverletter1.doc (see Figure 3.2).

It is essential to save your work on a regular basis. There is nothing more irritating than to lose documents you have spent time on because you didn't take the half a second to save them. Save your documents often and keep them in a folder of job-hunting letters. You will go to this folder time and time again during the job hunt.

By the way, if you are smart, once you are settled in a new position you will keep your online job-hunting folders. If you save all your templates, a couple of years down the road when you are ready for another step up the ladder of success, some of the drudgery of that job hunt will already have been accounted for.

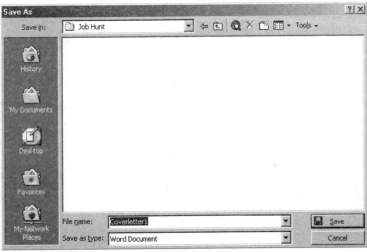

Figure 3.2 Saving the covering letter

Step 2

You need to make this covering letter suitable for e-mail. Just as with the examples in Chapter 2, there are two methods to accomplish this. For the sake of brevity, let's go through Method 1 but, if you prefer Method 2, simply follow the steps detailed in Chapter 2, replacing your CV with your covering letter.

Following Method 1, you need to set your margins to 60 characters per line, which equates to margins of about 1.7 to 1.75 inches on both the left and right sides (see Figure 3.3). You could count out 60 characters if that's easier.

Remember, you limit the number of characters per line so that the message does not 'wrap' to the next line or force the reader to scroll horizontally to read your message, a sure way to make yourself look incompetent.

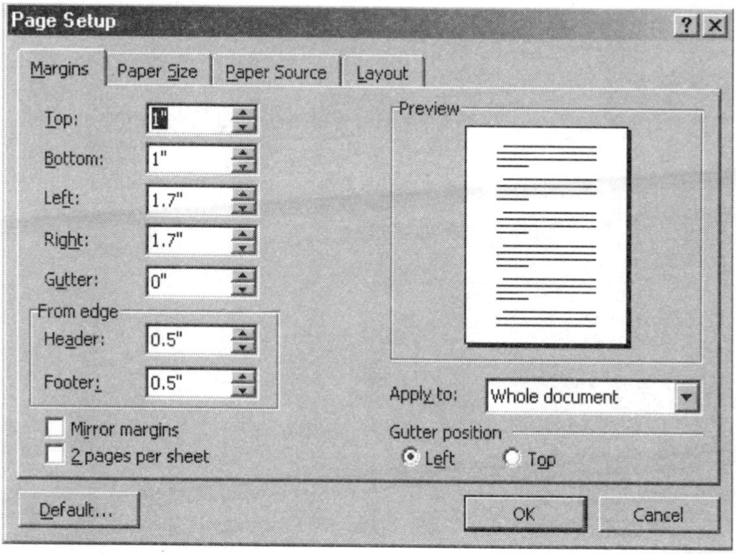

Figure 3.3 Setting the margins

51 University of Ulster LIBRARY

Step 3

Although you probably typed your covering letter using a default font, we need to make sure that your letters follow the same formats as your CV to assure readability. This means you need to use a 12-point font in Times New Roman or Courier style.

Go to the 'Edit' pull-down menu and choose 'Select All' (Cmd+A for Macintosh). Now you are going to change the font type and size. Choose 'Font' from the 'Format' pull-down menu and change the font type to Times New Roman or Courier and the size to 12 point (see Figure 3.4).

Step 4

Unlike with your traditional paper CV, you probably haven't put in any special effects such as underlining, bold

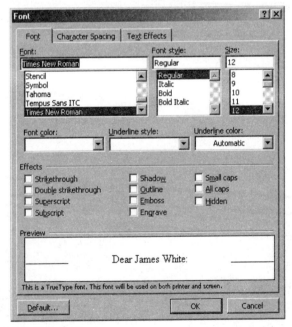

Figure 3.4 Setting the font

or italics. If you have, we need to get rid of them – remember we are creating a 'Text Only' message that will be sent via e-mail.

To do this you simply need to save your covering letter again. This time use the 'Save As' command but select the document type as 'Text Only' and rename. Let's call it TextCoverLetter1.doc (see Figure 3.5). When you do this, you will get a message box telling you that your formatting will change and asking you if you want to continue. You'll need to answer 'yes' because you do need to lose the formatting; that's what an ASCII or text-based covering letter is all about.

As you probably didn't have any special formatting in your covering letter you may not see many changes. That's OK – you still need to make sure. E-mails are so easy to use once you get the hang of them that it is all too easy to send out sloppy letters with misspellings, and punctuation and capitalization problems. As these communications are the very first impression the company gets of you, it is important that you are seen to be someone who pays attention to detail.

Figure 3.5 Saving in 'Text Only' format

Step 5

Your covering letter is now ready to go. Before you put the job hunt into high gear, get comfortable with a standard template creation procedure like we have described. You will be sending covering letters and CVs to a variety of contacts, and each of these will require a slightly different covering letter.

You will need covering letters for answering advertisements, responding to networking through friends and colleagues, submitting your CV to recruiters and headhunters, and submitting your CV to companies you've found through online research.

Each time the need for even a slightly different type of letter arises, make a template. The toughest thing about letter writing is getting the first draft down; it is much easier to adapt existing text. So make it easy on yourself: make templates.

What about other types of letters I might need?

As your job hunt progresses you will, at the very least, have the opportunity to send meeting confirmation, thank-you and follow-up notes. While you do not want to drown a prospective employer in electronic mail, sending such notes does help you stand out from the pack.

In filling a position a given employer might interview anywhere from 3 to 33 candidates. With every ensuing candidate after yourself, memory of your candidacy dims a little in the interviewer's mind. Sending thank-you notes and follow-up letters allows you to remind the interviewers of your existence. In advertising, they call this maintaining top-of-the-mind awareness.

Your follow-up notes can be a little longer because they are going to a person with whom you have already been in dialogue. With these follow-up letters:

- Identify who you are, when you met the person and the position it was in reference to.
- State how much you enjoyed the meeting and how excited you are about the opportunity. In a tightly run job race, where there is little to choose between two contenders, the offer always goes to the more enthusiastic candidate. Why? Because the enthusiasm, by inference, is a validation of the employer.
- Make an additional comment about a skill set or experience that applies to the candidacy that you didn't have the opportunity to reveal. Or if you didn't do a question justice, go back to it in the letter: 'Jon, when you asked me about..., I fear I was suffering from interview nerves. I actually have considerable expertise in this area. For example, I was involved with...' Then you finish the paragraph with 'Perhaps this is something we could address in our next meeting.'

Always end with a request for the next meeting: 'I am excited about your opportunity and my ability to make a real contribution. When will our next meeting be? I am looking forward to hearing from you. If not this week, perhaps I can call you early next week to set something up.'

In Chapter 5, we will show you how to put your CV and covering letter together in e-mail messages. But before we get there, in the next chapter we want to talk to you about protecting the confidentiality of your online job hunt.

four

How do I keep my online job hunt confidential?

I have heard horror stories about having your identity stolen and your employer finding out you are looking for another job. How can I protect my privacy on the Internet?

Personal privacy unfortunately becomes a real issue when you use the Internet for confidential matters like distributing your CV. The ease of electronic distribution means that many more people are going to see your CV than when you use more traditional methods. That's the good news. However, there is a downside: just as your ease of distribution is enhanced, so it becomes easier for anyone else to see and distribute, or otherwise tamper with, your professional identity. So take precautions to protect your privacy.

If you are gainfully employed, this is paramount. Studies show that upwards of 50 per cent of all companies either read employees' e-mail or track their Internet usage. This means not only should you not conduct your job hunt at the office but planning your next vacation or attending an auction should also be avoided. Some companies have even implemented programs to offer a 'finders' fee' if a staff member's CV appears online. This seems to be happening in the high-tech industries, as staff are terribly hard to find – and even harder to keep. All the same, be professional at work and, if you are employed, consider a confidential job-search attack.

The very ease of electronic distribution that makes online job hunting so attractive also means you have to develop some new behaviours to protect yourself. Using the Internet will maximize your productivity, but at the same time you must learn to manage and protect your online identity. This isn't a difficult thing to achieve. It is just a matter of understanding the rules of the game and setting up some behaviour protocols for yourself. In doing this for the benefit of your job hunt you will also learn to protect your identity in all other areas of your online life.

When you first go online you will automatically get an e-mail address. If you have Internet access from home, it is probably through a local ISP (Internet service provider) such as FreeServe, World Online or AOL. These accounts typically only come with one e-mail address, although many like FreeServe offer more. You should maintain this address for personal and family use, and set up new e-mail addresses and identities for your job hunt. We recommend this because you need to maintain clear separation between your personal and professional life, and your professional life and your job search. Your online job hunt will generate a vast amount of e-mail messages, and these can get lost or mishandled by family members, or you just might overlook them yourself.

Did you say e-mail addresses, as in more than one?

As you start a career you build experience in one specific area. However, after only a few years in a professional career you can probably read the appointments section of the newspaper and see that there are a number of different jobs that your experience would allow you to pursue. In effect you have the potential for multiple professional identities. Setting up separate e-mail accounts for each of these identities will allow you to keep things separate, and so you will be able to manage your job-hunting activities without confusion.

While you probably pay a monthly bill for your Internet access and initial e-mail account, these subsequent e-mail addresses needn't cost you another penny, as you will see as we move through this chapter.

What are the privacy issues I should be most concerned about?

If you are employed, you don't want a current employer to see your CV. It could cost you your job. Even if this isn't the case, it will almost certainly affect your standing in the company. There will be questions about which assignments you should get, and questions at performance and salary review time – all career complications that you can well do without. Don't dismiss this advice because you feel your boss is computer illiterate or too stupid. Almost all companies are using the Internet for recruitment purposes so it could just as easily be someone in human resources who stumbles across your unprotected online identity, while pursuing an online recruitment assignment.

While we are on the subject of privacy, there is the possibility of identity fraud – too much personal information on a CV can lead to your personal or professional identity being taken. Putting your home address and phone number can lead to junk mail and will increase the chances of getting telemarketing calls at home (and you know those always come just when you are sitting down to dinner or tuning in to the latest soap on TV).

Your professional identity is at risk when you list your

licence or certificate numbers on your CV – so don't, not ever. Someone could take those numbers, and their subsequent actions could result in your professional credibility being ruined. You can always supply the numbers in person during the interview process or when asked for them by a bona fide interested party.

Reverse spamming is another issue to be concerned about. Spamming is Internet slang for sending junk e-mail. Reverse spamming is when an electronic spider grabs your CV to redistribute, or the site you post to passes it on to another site.

> **electronic spider** A tool programmed to scour the Internet for certain types of information the 'spider owner' wants.

In your case, a telemarketing, direct mail or e-mail response company could well have spiders out looking for any documents that contain personal data and contact information. No big deal, you say. Well, will that be the case when your partner wants to know why you are getting all this e-mail from adult entertainment sites? Don't laugh. This has happened to one of the authors and, as you can imagine, it caused a major traumatic upheaval for all concerned. You can only stop these kinds of things happening if you take the proper steps to protect your online identity.

Can you give me some cut-and-dried rules to protect my privacy?

The vast majority of employment sites are reputable and make their best efforts to maintain happy and satisfied customers. Nevertheless, the entire online world is a wild new frontier and, as with any frontier, there are plenty of unscrupulous people around looking to make money by preying on the innocent and uninformed. Here are the steps you can take to protect your online privacy:

- Look for the site's privacy statement (every site has one – look for the small print at the bottom of the page) to understand what they say they will do on your behalf. Even though it doesn't guarantee that they will adhere to it, it's a start.
- Only post your CV to sites that password-protect the CV bank (this prevents spiders). Password protection allows the site to screen visitors electronically to make sure that only credible employers and recruiters get access to the CV database.
- Be sure you know who owns and operates the site. You should be able to find contact information for the owners and operators – it's just like doing business in the concrete world. You want to know with whom you are dealing. If they can't tell you who they are, don't post with them.
- Always, always, always make sure you can update and remove your posted CV whenever you want to. You do not want old and outdated information circulating about you, and if you do secure a position with a company that prohibits you posting a CV while employed, then you could have a new set of problems.
- Do not trust 'blocked' CV bank services. A blocked service is one where you can specify who you do not want to view your work CV. Just because a site claims it will block your current employer from seeing your CV, that doesn't mean it is fail-proof – do not take the chance. Instead, you will take the responsibility to protect your identity in the ways we will show you in this chapter.
- If you build and create your own Web site to post your CV and work samples, password-protect your own site as well, although we do not recommend this unless you are technologically adept enough to do it without the considerable time investment necessary to learn how. Always know who is taking a look at you, and retain the ability to block visitors you do not want – it is necessary

to take a proactive stance in managing your online presence.

- You should never put your national insurance number, driving licence number or professional licence number on your CV – either electronic or hard copy.
- You should only use your own e-mail addresses, not your employer's. Never download your secure e-mail to your office e-mail inbox either. Why? Three reasons:
  - Privacy issues within the workplace are in turmoil right now so your company may be viewing your mail, and your inbox is a security breach because others can read it.
  - You could accidentally leave the Internet browser open and someone could access your secure e-mail account.
  - Checking your secure e-mail account through your work computer could be traced back by a variety of tracking tools and software that companies use. This could be deemed inappropriate use of a work computer and Internet access for personal use on company time. So, play it safe; set up a secure e-mail address and only check it outside the workplace.

You will need at least one additional e-mail address to separate personal e-mail from professional e-mail. If you are going after more than one job you should consider having a separate address for each type of job; this will help you keep things organized. If your Internet service provider doesn't allow multiple e-mail addresses, you do have options. You can sign up for free e-mail through sites such as FreeServe, ClickAMail and AgencyCentral.

Many of the CV banks will give you a blind account for responses from their clients, but that will only help you with e-mail responses to your postings on those particular sites; you probably won't be able to receive mail from other sources with this option. Sometimes CV writers and career-counselling firms will furnish you with a numbered account that will protect your privacy in all online job-hunting endeavours. We'll go into the nuts and bolts of setting up free e-mail accounts next.

With an electronic CV, your e-mail address can replace most of your other contact information, although you may choose to keep your home telephone number on it. Remember the risk here is junk mail and telemarketing calls to your home. However, if this gives you confidentiality concerns, and it may if you are employed in a sensitive position, you can rent a voice mailbox for just a few pounds a month. You can use this voice mailbox as the contact telephone number for all your job-search activities until you are in communication with people to whom you want to reveal your personal identity and contact information.

How do I go about setting up multiple e-mail accounts to separate my personal and professional activities, and to protect my privacy?

Many online job-hunting sites and CV distribution services promise job-seeker confidentiality. This isn't enough. You can inadvertently reveal yourself through an unsecured e-mail address, or through information on the CV or covering letter that was not properly changed. Apart from that, sometimes the blocking mechanisms at the job site don't work as well as they were presented.

The first step towards online security is to get a confidential e-mail address. This is the equivalent of an espionage agent's drop box: it is a dead end that leads nowhere and to which only you have the key. Don't try to get by with your work or office e-mail – it is insecure and could cause problems if your e-mails were to be read by other parties. Neither should you trust the family e-mail address nor a friend's, as you can, and will, miss important messages.

You can easily set up a dedicated e-mail account for your

confidential job search. Just get yourself one of the free accounts that are offered by the likes of FreeServe, ClickAMail, AgencyCentral or any of the many other free e-mail sites – there are literally dozens of them and more popping up all the time. Once at the free e-mail site of your choice, follow the simple instructions for setting up an account; it takes less than five minutes. In fact, we'll show you how easy it is and give you a couple of suggestions along the way. Let's set up a new account using ClickAMail.

Once at the front page of ClickAMail, you will need to follow the instructions and enter your name. For the purpose of this example, let's use Jane Holmes from the CV sample we used in Chapter 2 (see Figure 4.1).

You always want to give yourself a professional e-mail address – remember, this is for use in your job search, not to exchange jokes with your friends. Don't use something like binky@clickamail.com or theman@clickamail.com. This site lists some suggested e-mail addresses based on your name. You should not use these if you are conducting a confidential job search, as that would defeat the purposes. So,

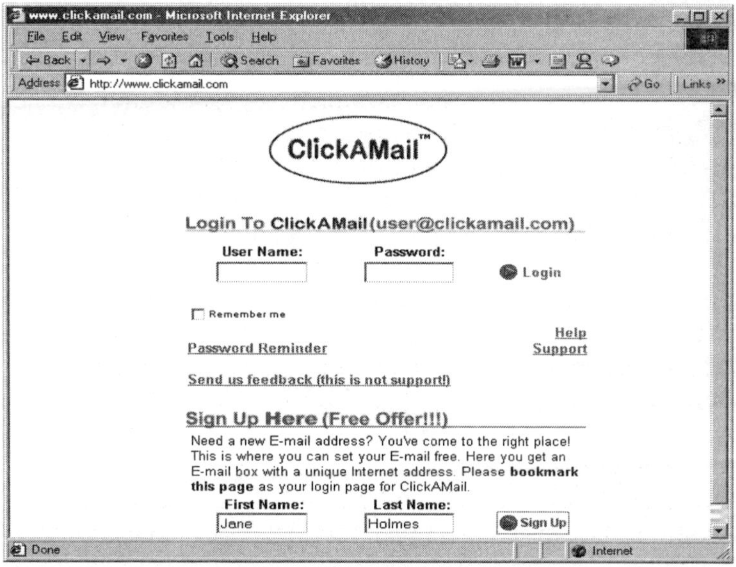

Figure 4.1 Setting up a free e-mail account

jane@clickamail.com is not a good choice for our example. Instead, let's create an account with some form of job title as part of the address such as newaccountant@clickamail.com or newauditor@clickamail.com as this will also help the recipients give focus to your communication from the first interaction (see Figure 4.2).

Now we've chosen an account name (sometimes called a user name) and you will need to choose a password. Sometimes the address or user name you want is not available. Just keep trying different combinations or words, or add a number as in newaccountant007.

Before you can use your new account, you will be asked to complete a short personal profile and to agree to the site rules and privacy statement (see Figure 4.3). This will include your agreeing to receive solicitations based on your profile. Remember the saying that nothing is really free?

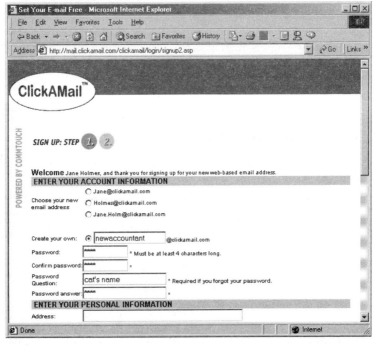

Figure 4.2 Creating an account name

These free e-mail accounts may not cost you money, but they can cost you in other ways. From your profile and account usage you will be sent a variety of marketing and sales pitches. Depending on the free account you choose, the number and frequency of this 'junk mail' will vary. As you complete your profile always read each screen carefully as you may be able to opt out of receiving some of the junk mail. While nothing is ever free, you can quickly and easily delete junk e-mails (spam) with a simple click of your mouse. The bottom line is that for the few junk e-mails you get, the benefit of a well-organized job search is worth it.

Now, having successfully set up our new e-mail account for our job search, you want to make sure you write down your address and password in a safe place. One of the best things about these free e-mail providers is that you can access your e-mail from any computer at any time. You

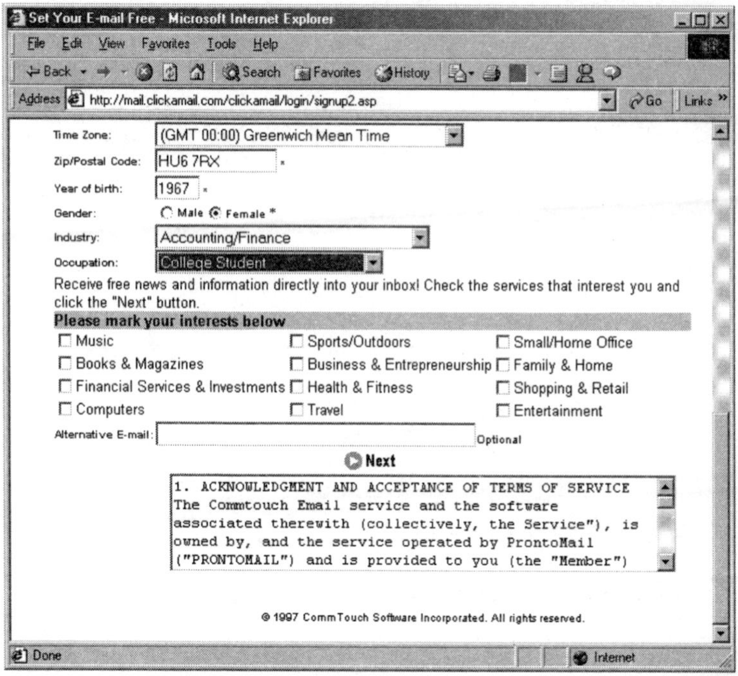

Figure 4.3 Completing set-up of the new account

simply go to the site's main page, in this case www.clicka-mail.com, and enter your user name and password (see Figure 4.4).

In our example, we enter 'newaccountant' and our password (in this case, a cat's name, milo) and here we are in our new mailbox (see Figure 4.5).

So there you have it: your first free e-mail account is set up and you have your first message – from the site's owners. There'll be more like that but soon you'll see job opportunities and messages from companies anxious to speak to you.

Figure 4.4 Accessing your e-mail

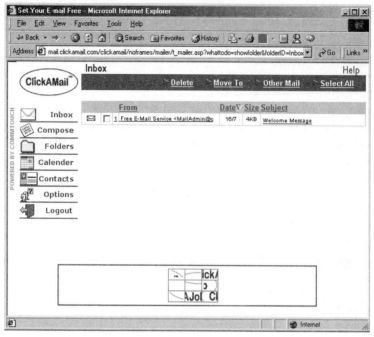

Figure 4.5 The new mailbox

Excellent. Now I have a secure e-mail address, but what about my CV? It still has my name and contact information on it; won't that compromise my confidentiality?

There is no point in having a secure Internet address and then blabbing about exactly who you are on the CV, so let's take a moment and revisit the information you have on your CV. Every hard copy CV gets passed hand to hand, and with the Internet's ease of transmission for electronic documents there is no telling where your electronic CV might end up. So once you have a secure, professional e-mail address, you need to sanitize your CV – based on the level of confidentiality you need to maintain.

What needs to be changed? For optimal security and for

every employed job seeker – all contact information (name, address, phone, fax, e-mail). Simply replace them with the dedicated e-mail address you created and refer to yourself as 'TopCandidate' or 'Job Seeker' or 'Confidential Accountant': you get the idea.

Remove current employer names, town or city and county. Replace these with a general description of the company and location. For example, if you worked for Fat Chance Technology in Middlesex, you could confidentially describe this as a 'leading technology company' in the Home Counties.

By changing current employer names and locations, you should be able to keep your job titles intact and easily protect your security; it usually isn't necessary to sanitize prior employer contact information. If you have a job title that is unique or in some way identified with a particularly visible company, it could be a clue as to who you are. In this case you should change it to a more generic or common title. Be sure to indicate that you listed a position equivalent, for example Sales Director (position equivalent title).

One last word on CVs in this context: many job boards will tell you their software creates the perfect CV, which is invariably not the case. So don't count on the job boards or CV distribution services to help you create the perfect confidential CV; do this yourself.

If you follow these simple guidelines, your job search will be entirely confidential, and you will have taken one further step towards better control and effective management of your career.

Sometimes I get incomprehensible e-mails. How will I know if my e-mails are getting to the right place and if anyone can read them when they get there?

Before you start looking at the job and CV banks and getting your CV out into cyberspace, you need to make sure all your work is going to have the desired impact. There is no point in sending out e-mails that can't be read, or CVs that the recipient can't open, or won't open for fear of viruses. So now we are quickly going to address how to use e-mail effectively: using proper subject lines, attachments or no attachments, electronic signatures and electronic stationery.

E-mail is fast – in fact it can be instantaneous – and when you e-mail directly to a contact from a job posting or from a company Web site, you know precisely to whom it's going. However, it won't get opened and read unless it is received in a format that the recipient is comfortable in opening. You can safely assume that, unless specifically stated, an employer expects a text CV to be sent in the body of the e-mail message – pasted into the body of the message, not as an attachment. If you are not sure what an attachment is, that's fine; we'll be showing you exactly what one is and how to do an attachment in just a few paragraphs.

How do I get my CV into the body of the e-mail message?

E-mail communications aren't fancy in any way; in fact the restrictions of the technology mean that most e-mail communications are going to look pretty much alike. Consequently, you won't be able to impress the recipients with that beautifully laid-out paper CV that we have all become used to over the years. That's the bad news. The good news is that the majority of the British workforce has already declared that it has no intention of ever going online. Now because you are using an electronic approach you stand apart. Employers are eagerly awaiting communications from people like you: one of the few technologically adapted in the New World of work.

Here's the step-by-step of how to take that CV created in your word-processing program and get it into an e-mail:

1. Remember the ASCII CV we created in Chapter 2?

That's what we need. We created two versions, one in our word-processing program and one in our simple text-based WordPad program. It doesn't matter which one you use; the result will be the same. So let's open our text CV (see Figure 4.6). (Note: now that Jane has her new e-mail account, she has incorporated this into her CV.)

2. You are probably an old hand at this by now, but we need to 'Copy' the entire document. We do this by choosing 'Select All' from the 'Edit' pull-down menu (Cmd+A for Macintosh) and then 'Copy' from the 'Edit' pull-down menu or Ctrl+C for Windows (Cmd+C for Macintosh) (see Figure 4.7).

3. We need to go to our new e-mail account and create a new message. You can move or toggle between programs by clicking on the appropriate icons on your desktop or by using alt+tab on your keyboard. A message box describing the program or document will appear in the centre of the screen; simply tap the 'tab' key while depressing the 'alt' key until the program of your choice appears and then release both keys.

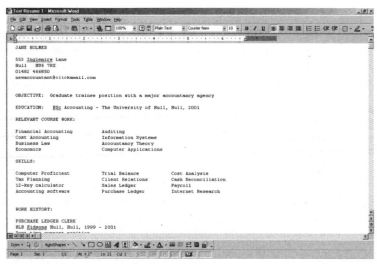

Figure 4.6 Opening the text CV

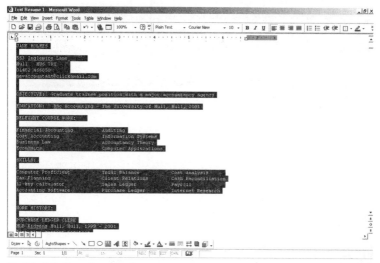

Figure 4.7 Copying the document

We create a new message by choosing the 'Compose' menu option on our e-mail server (see Figure 4.8).

4. Simply place the cursor into the body of the e-mail message and paste your text CV by choosing 'Paste' from the 'Edit' pull-down menu or Ctrl+V for Windows (or Cmd+V for Macintosh) (see Figure 4.9).

5. Carefully enter the e-mail address, making sure you have it correct. Always use a powerful subject line when sending an e-mail – not just job-related e-mails but every e-mail you send should have a clear, concise and professional subject line. It allows the receiver to know immediately who you are and what you want (see Figure 4.10). The subject line you use is like the headline for a newspaper article, where its purpose is to grab the reader and draw him or her into the body of the article. With your e-mail, the subject line pulls the reader into opening the CV. Just like a headline, it should be short and relate to the body of the text you want the reader to examine: in this case it is your CV. With e-mail this is especially important, because everyone gets lots of junk mail so much of it gets deleted without ever being read.

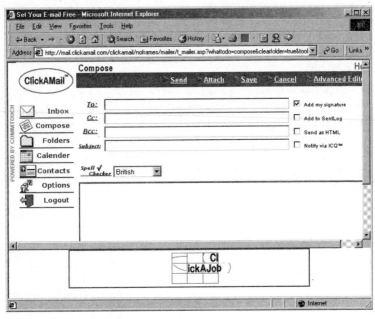

Figure 4.8 Choosing the 'Compose' option

Figure 4.9 Pasting the CV

Try lines like:

Top Sales Professional
Excellent Database Administrator
Superior Thoracic Surgeon

When your e-mail is delivered into an inbox the recipient will see whom it is from and what it is about. You will notice that the subject line and the e-mail address complement each other, and both provide different and enticing information for the reader – just like the headline we used as an analogy:

Subject	From
Superior Surgeon	thoracic@clickamail.com

I can't imagine a hospital administrator in the world who wouldn't open this e-mail.

Now we want you to do a few trial runs with this. Cut and paste your text CV into the body of half a dozen e-mails, try out different subject lines and then send them to yourself at every different e-mail address you have created and to a few friends. In the message to your friends tell them

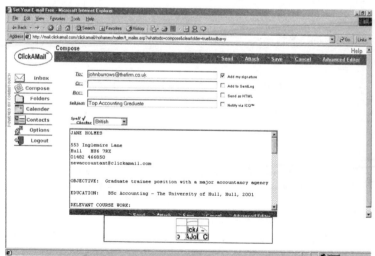

Figure 4.10 Subject line

you are trying this out and want them to let you know that they received and could read your entire communication. If possible, have them print it for you so you can see exactly what the receiver sees – sometimes it may surprise you.

But my CV looks so much more professional in MS Word; can't I send it this way?

Your word-processing program allows you to format your CV in a way that reflects the traditional paper document. The problem is that when you cut and paste this into the body of an e-mail message all the formatting is lost, and it looks just like any other e-mail message in its layout.

To retain the 'pretty' format created by your word-processing program you can't put it into the body of the e-mail; instead you have to send it as an attachment. This is rather like sending someone a wrapped gift with a card on the outside. That person will read the card first and then open the gift. It will work the same way when you send an e-mail with your CV as a separate document attached to the e-mail.

> **attachment** A document or file added to an e-mail message.

Typically employers do not like attachments. There are two major reasons for this. First of all, there is no guarantee that recipients have the same word-processing program you are using, so they may not be able to open it and, even if they can, perhaps all the neat formatting will be lost. Also, e-mails are a major way that viruses are spread from computer to computer. Consequently the company may have a policy against opening such documents, or a particular manager may simply have had a bad virus experience from having done so. Unless you are specifically requested to send your CV as an attachment, send your CV within the body of the message.

Nevertheless, there will be times when you will have the opportunity to send a formatted CV as an attachment, and because they look so much better you want to be able to do so when the opportunity arises.

There are two types of attachments. First, ASCII or text attachments are the CVs we created in the previous chapter using Notepad or a similar text-based program. These are ideal, as essentially any computer can open them, but, as we have said, they are not graphically arresting. Second, formatted attachments are the CVs you created using your word processor like Microsoft Word, WordPerfect, etc. Remember, in order for employers to open your formatted CV, they must have the same word-processing software as you. Otherwise you risk the chance of them not being able to open it or the formatting being messed up. Only send a formatted CV when the employer has asked for one and specified a preferred program. If you do not have that program, stick to a text or ASCII CV to be safe.

Figure 4.11 Selecting the attachment document

Now here's how you send an attachment. Each e-mail program is a little different, so follow the screen instructions carefully. Start by selecting the attachment icon or menu choice from the e-mail message you created (see Figure 4.11).

You will need to find the document you need to send (see Figure 4.12). You do this by browsing your computer's directory. It is always easiest if you have all of your job-related documents in one place and then you can quickly find what you need.

Although e-mail programs and features vary, you should be able to verify that the file is attached. Often an icon with the file name appears or the file name is listed as an attached document (see Figure 4.13).

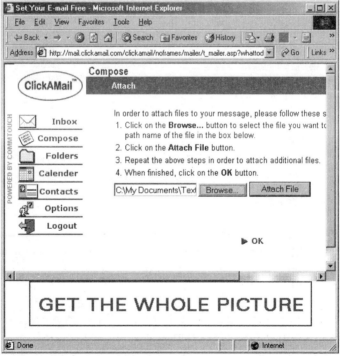

Figure 4.12 Finding the document

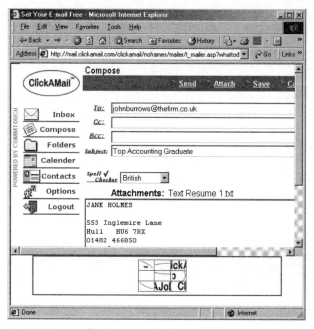

Figure 4.13 Verifying the file is attached

I've received a couple of e-mails that had the sender's actual signature on them. This was different and really got my attention. How do I do it?

Creating an electronic signature is easy, and it is a nice touch that might well help you stand out. Nice touch or not, using an electronic signature is not something you have to do; it's a plus that can't hurt.

If you are in a high-tech profession or know that the person to whom you are sending the CV and covering letter is very computer-savvy, then you should go ahead and do it. How? It's easy and there are really two types of signatures. One is the actual signature as shown in Figure 4.14; the other is a text-only (see Figure 4.15) – more or less a

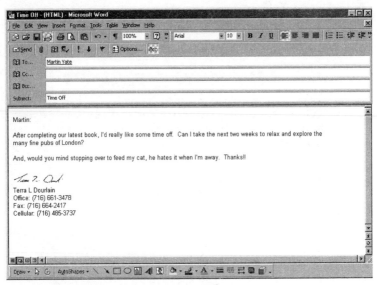

Figure 4.14 Actual signature on an e-mail

Figure 4.15 Text signature on an e-mail

professional sign-off or letter ending with the contact information and text of your choice.

These are the steps:

1. You need to be aware of the capabilities of your e-mail program as you may or may not be able to create this option. Many of the free programs do not offer these advanced options. If you are using your own ISP, then you probably use an e-mail program such as Microsoft Outlook.

   In Microsoft Outlook you would choose the 'Mail Format' menu choice from the 'Options' menu (see Figure 4.16). This will take you through a complete set-up process that will allow you to choose what complete text you want to accompany your signature and whether that signature is a picture of your real one or text only (see Figure 4.17).

2. If you want to add your actual signature to your

Figure 4.16 'Options' menu in Microsoft Outlook

Figure 4.17 Choosing your signature

e-mails, then you will need to create a file that is a picture of your signature. To do that, you will need to sign your name on a blank piece of paper and then scan the sheet using a scanner. Many new computers are being sold with simple scanners because it is all the craze to scan family pictures. But if you are in a technical profession, you probably have a scanner or easy access to one. If you are just interested and think you have the potential to be a true techno geek, ask your friends or even the local copy shop – they'll probably have a scanner for you.

3. Once scanned, save the file as 'Personal Signature' or a similar recognizable file name. You would then insert this file into the signature text of the e-mail. Be aware that this is like adding a picture or graphic to every single e-mail you send so it could slow down delivery if either the sender or receiver has a slow connection.

What about personalized e-mail stationery? That would make my message stand out too, wouldn't it?

Yes, it would, but there are caveats. Stationery is a fancy way to customize your e-mail messages (see Figure 4.18), but it is not always a good idea in a job search unless you know the receiver will be impressed and needs to be. As scanning software is typically applied to the message, stationery could complicate the employer's process and hurt your chances. This is a personal judgement call on your part.

Examples of circumstances where electronic stationery is likely to make a positive statement about your candidacy

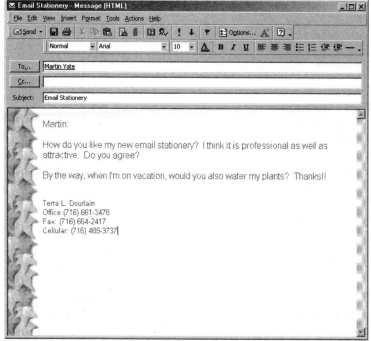

Figure 4.18 Personalized e-mail stationery

might include your being in a high-tech, graphic arts or design field. In such instances you are strutting your stuff professionally, and the recipient is more likely to have the software that can handle the more sophisticated layout.

Creating stationery is a function of some, but not all, e-mail programs. Typically the programs come with a variety of installed options (see Figure 4.19), but you could always add your own, using pictures or graphics you have created. Again, high use of graphics can slow down delivery, so be considerate when applying these techniques; you don't want to frustrate recipients by making them wait too long for the e-mail to load and open.

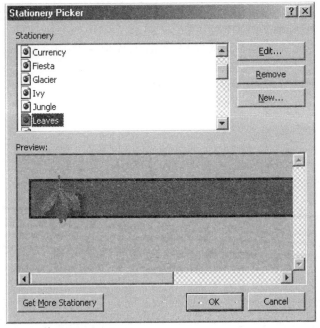

Figure 4.19 Choosing stationery

How do I know if people are getting my customized e-mails and can read my formatted CV?

You will need to do some dry runs just like you did with text pasted into the body of the e-mail. Practise sending formatted CVs as attachments, with covering letters, stationery and signatures, to friends and family, and between the various secure e-mail accounts you have set up. In fact, if you can find six people to receive your tests as well as e-mails sent to yourself to and from your various e-mails accounts, that would be ideal. Ask your test receivers to print and show you what exactly they received. You want to make sure that you are attaching and sending documents correctly and that what you send is what is actually received. If you add bells and whistles like electronic signatures and electronic stationery, you must go through the same dry-run procedure with each enhancement.

Once you have completed all these e-mail checks, there is just one more to do and you'll be 'ready to go'. Send your CV via fax to six friends as well. Ask them to print out and return a hard copy version of what was received. Here is the issue with faxing – many of us fax from our computers and not from a paper fax machine. We've seen CVs and covering letters that appear to come from a spouse or child, and received faxes where the spacing is incredibly off and the sender appears to have paid no attention to detail. Just like e-mail options, many fax programs allow the user to set up options that indicate the sender (which may not be you) or automatically send a fax covering letter (again, it may not have you as the person sending it). So, ask your friends to give you their feedback and see if they can catch any glitches.

Yes, it will take a little time to do this but, once you are confident that things are working properly, you can try it in the real world. The result you get is likely to be an avalanche of interview activity. In today's world your e-mail and fax communications create the employer's first impression, and we all know how important first impressions are. The message here is: learn to walk before you try to run.

As you progress in organizing your online job hunt, you will see that at this point you have confidential CVs, covering letters and e-mail accounts. The next steps are to look at some of the top sites to get a clear understanding of how to navigate around career sites, and to decide on what type of job hunt you will implement. That's what we are going to address in the next chapter.

five

What are the best career sites and how do I use them?

So, how do I find a job on the Internet?

Now that you have all the tools, your electronic CV, electronic covering letter templates and dedicated job-search e-mail accounts, this chapter will take you on an expedition of the Internet. You will learn:

- the different types of job boards;
- how to decipher an online job advertisement;
- how to respond to an online job advertisement;
- how to use a job board search engine effectively;
- how to post your CV into a CV bank;
- how to have jobs delivered to you;
- how to find a company Web site and submit your CV directly to that company.

As always, we will do this without overwhelming you with technical jargon.

Let's start by taking a look at these job boards. We've already mentioned Appendix A. We've done the most comprehensive research to date to compile a list of job sites for you – more than 1,000. This is your 'head start' on your competition. But how best to use these job boards in your job search is the task at hand now.

You may have heard of Fish4Jobs (www.fish4jobs.com), ClickAJob (www.clickajob.com) and Gis-a-Job (www.gis-a-job.com) – just to name a few. There are literally thousands of job boards on the Web with more popping up every day and on some days just as many leaving or merging with other sites. To say that the job board market is volatile would be an understatement. In fact, during the course of the research we conducted for this book, 50 per cent of what we initially thought of as our top 10 have shut down or merged with other sites. So be prepared for sites to change or disappear, and do not ever forget to keep looking for new sites; you will of course learn how to do this within the chapter.

So what job board is best?

The one where you find your dream job. Honestly, it could be on any job board. Not all job boards are created equally, and no one should rate job boards solely by the number of positions they post (in fact, we'll list our top 10 for you – see Chapter 6). Job boards come in all shapes and sizes and flavours; they all have different features and services they feel will appeal to their users.

There are different types of job boards and different motives that power the management of these boards. For the most part, all job boards are free for job seekers to search, but understanding the 'why' behind the job board will help you understand and qualify the information and services provided.

Job boards and banks are generally broken down into five types:

- the majors – large general sites;
- industry- or job-type-specific sites;
- geographic-specific sites;
- association job sites or minority-focused sites;
- company Web sites and career centres.

Online job postings are essentially an electronic extension of the classified section of newspapers. That means that companies pay to have jobs posted, and the higher the readership – the number of people viewing the jobs – or the more focused the readership, the more they pay. Let's talk for a moment about each of these types of job boards and get an idea of why they do what they do.

Most of the large or, as we refer to them, the majors operate just like electronic newspapers. Examples would be WorkThing.com (www.workthing.com) (owned by the *Guardian* and *Observer* newspapers) and Monster UK (www.monster.co.uk) (owned by the world's largest recruitment advertising firm). There is absolutely nothing wrong with these sites. In fact, they are great places to start any online job search as they offer many great services in addition to job boards. The only downfall is that they are there to please the masses so the jobs cover many (but not necessarily all) job fields and geographies. So if you are looking for a needle in a haystack, you may look long and hard here and still never find what you are looking for.

A second type of job board is one that is specific to a job function or industry. These sites come in many sizes but most are medium to small. These sites are of special use to you in your job hunt as, in addition to jobs, they often feature career advice, plus trends and links to valuable networking resources such as associations, seminars and continuing education. Good examples of these types of sites include AccountingWeb (www.accountingweb.co.uk) and MedJobsUK.com (www.medjobsuk.com).

Industry- or job-focused sites are typically fuelled by two different types of site owners. The first kind of site is managed by an industry-specific information or service provider. AccountingWeb is a great example of this. By providing information, continued education and other services, AccountingWeb has increased its visibility and service level by adding a job board. On the other hand, MedJobsUK.com represents the more popular type of management typical to industry job boards. That is the recruitment or headhunting industry. These are still free sites to you but the motive is to place you in a vacancy for one of their fee-paying clients. These sites will often have a lengthy registration process in order for them to learn as much about you as possible, either for a specific job today or to have you on file for a future client's needs.

Again, there is nothing wrong with this type of site – in fact they can prove to be incredible useful – but it is important to understand the motivation behind the site so that you react and analyse the information to your benefit. We'll take you through the registration process later in this chapter, but suffice it to say that the information you give a site will not only affect your privacy but also your ability to attract the attention of the HR person or recruiter. Industry-specific sites are so important to your successful online job search that we have identified over 750 such sites across 26 different industry categories to help guide you.

A third type of job board is the geographic-specific board. If you are in the position that you cannot or will not relocate, these local job boards can be a great asset. As they are typically small and often managed by local newspapers or independent owners, new sites are popping up as fast as existing ones are failing. A couple of examples of these include: MerseyWorkplace (www.merseyworkplace.com) and yorkjobs (www.yorkjobs.co.uk). Just as the names imply, these sites are specific to these geographic areas. While all of the major sites will allow you to search based on geographic considerations, often these local sites have a closer pulse on the local job market and some employers are turning to them for online recruitment services.

Of course the complete opposite of the locally geographic site is the international site. Often the front page of these sites will allow you to select a region or country. Jobs-at.com (www.jobs-at.com) is an example, as they have coverage in the UK, United States, Canada and Australia, while JobPilot (www.jobpilot.co.uk) lists over 100,000 vacancies across Europe.

The fourth type of site is one managed by a professional organization or minority support group. The British Pharmacological Society at www.bps.ac.uk and the Disability Times online (www.youreable.com) are two fine examples of associations and special needs groups addressing career issues for their members. Often these sites can offer more personal and professional support than huge numbers of job openings, but managing your career is a lifetime commitment and networking with others in your situation is invaluable. Companies advertising on minority sites can offer your candidacy a special edge, because not only is the employer looking for someone with your professional skills set but it is also looking for someone with your minority profile.

The last type of site is the company site and job bank. Typically the larger companies will dedicate a portion of their Web site to the recruitment process. Siemens UK (www.siemens.co.uk) is a great example of a corporation recruiting directly from their own company site. In addition to a searchable job bank, most company job pages offer detailed information about the company, its benefits, long-term vision, biographies of senior management and recent press releases. In terms of interview preparation, a company Web site can offer a plethora of information. Later in this chapter you will learn how to find a company's Web site and, once there, how to find their jobs and contact information.

How do I use these job search engines?

Now, you already have a huge head start on your competition because of the great resources and 1,000-plus job sites we've found for you. But don't think you can just go crazy and bolt through that list. Your time is valuable, and you've already taken the effort to have your electronic CV and covering letters ready to go so take the time to understand these job search engines and how to use them effectively.

First, you need to determine what type of site you are using: a major, geographic-specific, association or what. This will affect the type of returns you can expect and how you use the various services the site offers.

Start by reading the front page of the site thoroughly. Do not start clicking from page to page immediately. The front page is your best information source to determine what services the site offers, and is a link to who owns the site. Let's take a look at the front page of Fish4Jobs (www.fish4jobs.co.uk) (see Figure 5.1).

The very front page offers a large list of options for job hunters such as finding a job, setting up a personal folder to store and receive job information via e-mail, career services, psychometric tests and advice across many functions, just to name a few. Additionally you see a link titled 'About fish4' at the very bottom of the left-hand menu. This is

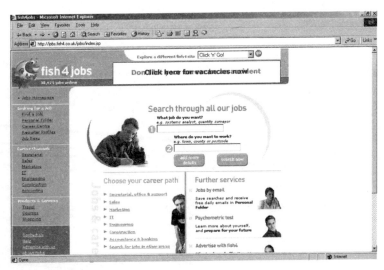

Figure 5.1 Front page of Fish4Jobs

Figure 5.2 About fish4

where you will find the description of the site owners (see Figure 5.2).

From this information we can determine that the owners of this site are a marketing services firm that manages two other sites providing services to consumers. It is safe to assume that you will be asked if they can add your name to certain e-mailing and marketing lists. Here's the bottom line – if this site has a good number of jobs for you, then use it. You can get out of the mailing lists easily enough and, as they are dependent upon you for traffic on this board, you are not likely to get overwhelmed with marketing messages.

Now although this site offers many tools and services, we are going to focus on searching the job postings for the moment. Let's assume that you are comfortable with the company managing the site and the privacy policy regarding any information you submit to or through the site.

Each site has different features so do not be afraid to try them out and determine which ones are of most value to you. This particular site allows you to conduct a job search immediately from the front page, but the options on the search criteria are limited, so this may or may not be the best way to use this site. You will notice in the left-hand menu a choice to 'Find a Job'.

As you are a new user to this site, it is best to search the entire job bank, so you choose the link for 'Find a Job'. This leads you to the site's job search engine, which will allow you to fine-tune your search in a variety of categories. Again each site is a little different so explore the options and how they affect the results you get. On this site you can narrow your search based on job title, keywords, industry sector, location, position type (contract, permanent, etc), salary and date the job was posted (see Figure 5.3).

Let's go back to our CV examples from Chapter 2, and

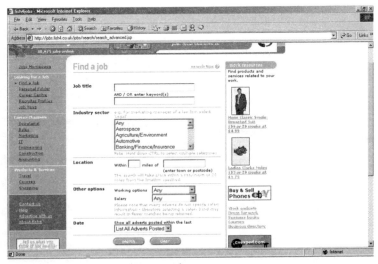

Figure 5.3 Fine-tuning your search

you can see how Joseph Brown, our Manufacturing Manager and Chemical Engineer, should use this search engine. Here's a key search tip – the first time you search on any site, keep your search as broad as possible. The reason for this is simple: the more specific you make your search, the fewer matches you will get in return. You do not want to get an unfavourable opinion of a job bank just because they couldn't meet all of your criteria. Keep your search general at first and then narrow it down. This gives you a feeling for the depth of the jobs in the database and therefore an idea of whether your perfect job could ever be there.

So, on your first search attempt, you keep your criteria broad. In Joe's situation, we are going to list the position title 'Manufacturing Manager' as our only criterion (see Figure 5.4).

This will give you an idea on how many manufacturing jobs in general this site has, and is therefore a reflection of its reach into this type of job market. By clicking the 'search' button on the bottom of the page, you are asking the search engine to search its database for all matches. The result is shown in Figure 5.5.

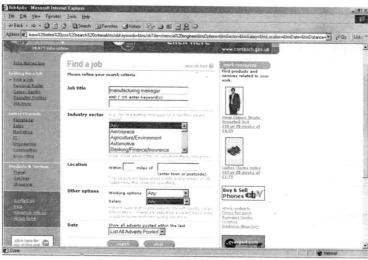

Figure 5.4 First search attempt

Figure 5.5 First search results

Now, when you get your results, don't go crazy and start clicking through the jobs looking for your perfect match. Just like when you entered the job site, take a moment to look at the results page – there is good information here. The best news for Joe is that this site has 5,812 matches for 'Manufacturing Manager'. You can see that by the sentence right above the first job match returned: 'The following are 1–10 of the 5812 jobs that match your search.' The bad news is that Joe had better not waste his time reading through all of these – instead let's narrow his search criteria.

We can do this by hitting the back button on our Internet browser or by looking for the 'amended search' link offered above the search results. Now remember, each site is different, but these menu options and techniques are common to all.

So, let's add criteria to Joe's search to narrow his results (see Figure 5.6). Because of Joe's substantial experience and desire to stay in the food and beverage industries, he is utilizing the keywords 'food' and 'beverage'. Joe is also using the industry sector search categories and has chosen two.

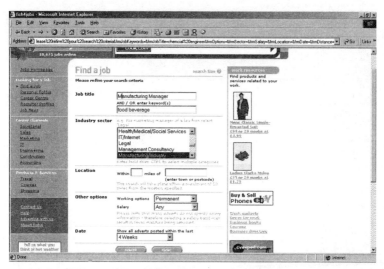

Figure 5.6 Refining the search criteria

This is typically done by holding down the control key on your keyboard ('Ctrl') while using your mouse to select the categories from the search engine. Joe chose both the engineering and manufacturing/industry selections.

As geography is not an issue, and Joe is willing to relocate as he has no children and is leasing a flat, he made no geographically restricting choices. Joe did add the job type of 'permanent' to his criteria, as he is not interested in a consulting position, and has limited the results to the last four weeks. Joe has also left the salary criterion open. Often salary is a huge factor in job search results yet it is one that is very negotiable and one that many firms do not list or simply list with a wide salary range on their job postings. So it is advisable that you carefully use or avoid using salary as a search engine criterion.

Joe's new results are much closer to the job he is looking for and more manageable (see Figure 5.7).

With the addition of the many search criteria, the number of matches has dropped to 586. Joe could continue this

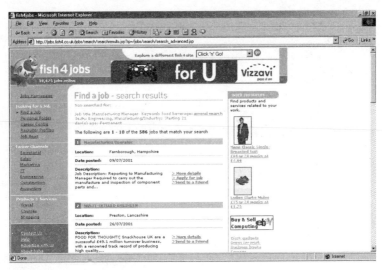

Figure 5.7 Refined search results

process or take a few minutes to view the first job posting returns and see how close the matches are.

Each site's search engine will be slightly different in operation. One way of quickly understanding the nuances of each search engine is to read its 'searching tips' or 'search help' advice. Fish4Jobs offers this information through a link right on the top of the search engine page. It is called 'search tips' and leads you to the page shown in Figure 5.8.

To show further the difference in search engines, let's discuss another type of search engine called a 'meta' engine. You'll see in the next few paragraphs that this is not a difficult term.

> **meta search engine** A search engine that takes your search criteria, searches not only its own database but also the databases from many different sites and gives you the results all at once.

Let's start by visiting the popular site ClickAJob (www.clickajob.com). This site claims to be the largest searchable human resource portal in the UK.

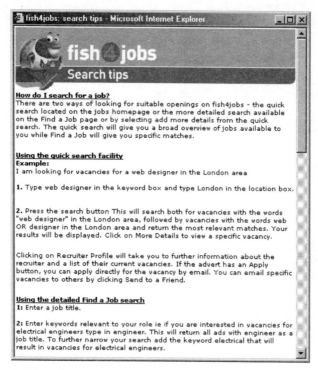

Figure 5.8 Search tips

> **portal** A Web site that is dedicated to providing information on one specific topic and accomplishes that through collecting and integrating information from other sites.

ClickAJob is a portal because it is a job site and has a ton of great information on the topic of jobs and careers. It also has a ton of jobs. What makes ClickAJob unique and of interest in your job search is that not only is it a portal but its job engine actually collects jobs from other job sites.

A simple search for a Sales Manager position on ClickAJob produces the results shown in Figure 5.9.

What is of particular interest is the column on the far right side. As you can see, these results came not only from the ClickAJob site but also from the Total Jobs and

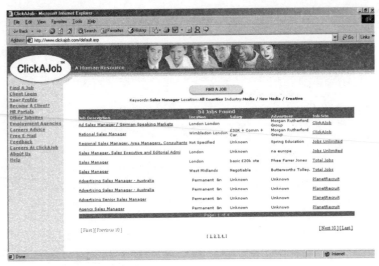

Figure 5.9 Search for a Sales Manager position

PlanetRecruit sites as well. Essentially, using a meta site is a way to search many sites at once, but do not confuse that with searching all the sites at once or doing it as well as it possibly can be done. Any meta site can only search other sites that it has agreed to share information with – not all sites all over the Internet.

Listed in Appendix A you will find many meta sites we've discovered for you. Take the time to read each one so you know what sites each meta site is searching and, if any of those sites return several jobs for you, then go directly to them. Obviously such a site is a good match for you so utilize it directly and make use of all of its services.

How do I use keywords in search engines?

From the first chapter in this book we have emphasized the concept of keywords. The reason for that is simple – it is keywords that drive search engines to give accurate results to your request, and they can therefore be immensely

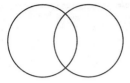

Figure 5.10 Overlapping circles

valuable assets in your job search. Search engines use Boolean search logic (George Boole is the person credited with the concept). Appendix C offers all the details so let's keep this simple. Boolean search logic is a kind of maths (and you told your maths teacher you'd never need that stuff in real life!). It's those overlapping circles of what things are exclusive or inclusive (see Figure 5.10).

What we are talking about here is (mathematical) '+' or (English) 'AND', for example keyword 1 AND keyword 2 must appear in the job to be returned as a match. Take this a step further and you can eliminate or narrow results by eliminating jobs if certain words appear – (mathematical) '-' or (English) 'NOT'. Some sites take both the maths version and the English, but be sure to read the rules.

Let's demonstrate this by using the example of an engineer. Different types of engineers have very different training and job skills. So, searching a job bank for engineer positions would return all types of engineers, a real pain if you are a Chemical Engineer.

Let's go to StepStone (www.stepstone.co.uk). StepStone is a leading UK and European job site that features a very strong Boolean search engine. In fact, StepStone offers a great help screen to assist you in understanding this concept, as do many sites – so always read every site's search tips.

First, let's select the option to conduct a Boolean keyword search on the StepStone job bank (see Figure 5.11). Some sites will combine this with other categories such as location, salary, industries, etc; it doesn't matter what – the logic is all the same.

Figure 5.11 Selecting a keyword search option

After selecting to do a keyword search we keep it simple and only enter the keyword 'Engineer'. No other categories, locations or other limitations for the purpose of this exercise are considered.

Five hundred job postings came back (see Figure 5.12), and look at the different types of jobs in just the first few results: Support Engineers, Software Engineer, Hardware Engineer – but what about the Chemical Engineers? You could get lost in this sea of engineering jobs and never find one for you. The beauty of Boolean keyword searching is that it allows you to narrow the results using keywords specific to you.

So, let's use our Boolean power and narrow this result. Let's add 'Chemical' to our search requirements. The Boolean search request would look like this: 'Engineer AND Chemical'. This means that all the job postings returned have to have both of those words in them.

What a difference: just by adding the keyword 'Chemical', we dropped our results from 500 to just 17 (see Figure 5.13). Now although 17 might seem manageable, if you were using several search engines in your job hunt

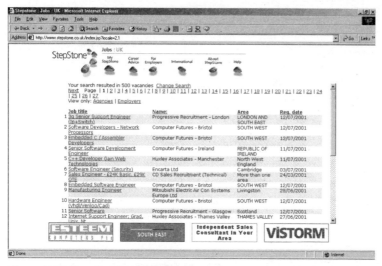

Figure 5.12 Results of an 'Engineer' search

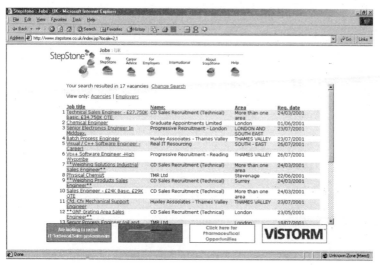

Figure 5.13 Results of an 'Engineer AND Chemical' search

(which is recommended), then limiting pointless returns could be a key to saving a lot of time. Not all Chemical Engineers are interested in the sales aspect of the position, so let's assume that we are not interested in a job that involves any aspect of sales. You should use Boolean logic to eliminate all jobs that have to do with sales. The Boolean search string would look like this: 'Engineer AND Chemical NOT Sales'.

The results are even narrower – only seven jobs were returned (see Figure 5.14). Not all of these will be perfect matches. Just as you added many keywords to your CV to get attention, companies and recruiters do the same. Even if the job is not a perfect match for you, they want to raise your awareness of their firm as you never know what the future holds. Applying the same philosophy, you may want to consider whether it is a good company but the wrong job. Maybe they have a job for you on the company Web site. It also wouldn't be a bad idea to send the company your CV anyway; just because they aren't advertising doesn't mean they may not be looking.

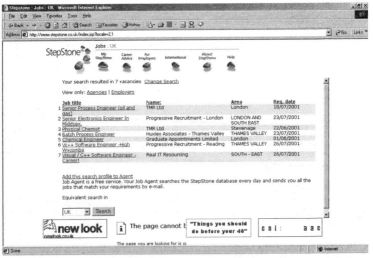

Figure 5.14 Results of an 'Engineer AND Chemical NOT Sales' search

How do I know if an online job advert is for a real job?

Before you search for jobs you look over the job site to determine the owner and privacy considerations of the site. As such you should be fairly confident that you've found jobs that are real and available.

There are a few 'red flags' or indicators that you should consider before blindly responding to any ad. First, look for contact information. It may not be the company directly if they have hired a recruiter, but there should be fairly complete contact information including a company or recruitment company name, a contact person or code and e-mail, fax, phone and/or postal information. And second, if most of this contact information is lacking and it is accompanied by a very vague job description and flexible job location, you may have a dud on your hands. Bottom line, use common sense and, before you send out anything about yourself, feel comfortable about whom you are sending it to and for what specific position.

Now that I can find jobs and search job engines, how do I respond? How do I send them my CV?

That is why we prepared ahead of time. As you saw when we were searching those few job boards, finding a job posting is not a problem – there are plenty of matching opportunities for you. In the olden days, that meant a lot of printing, signing, addressing and licking envelopes. In today's world, just a few clicks and we are on our way.

Let's go back to one of the other CVs we put together in Chapter 2 – that of Jane Holmes. Jane was the new graduate with a degree and a little experience in accounting. At this point in her career she is open to experience and variety, but wants to move to Peterborough to be close to her boyfriend.

Jane has been using the search techniques demonstrated earlier in this chapter and quickly has results. She went to TopJobs.co.uk (www.topjobs.co.uk), which features a section specifically for new graduates, and is pleased with her search results (see Figure 5.15).

Specifically Jane was interested in the job for a Trainee Chartered Accountant in Peterborough, which was listed by the accounting firm Saffery Champness. To view more details of this job posting, she clicked on the job title (see Figure 5.16).

Just a few paragraphs ago we discussed how to determine the validity of a job opening. This particular job posting clearly states what company the job is from, offers a description of that organization and even offers links to the company Web site and corporate information from links in the upper right-hand corner. The bottom portion of the job posting offers contact and additional information (see Figure 5.17).

The job posting lists requirements of the job applicant including personal traits as well as educational and experience requirements. Although the contact information is

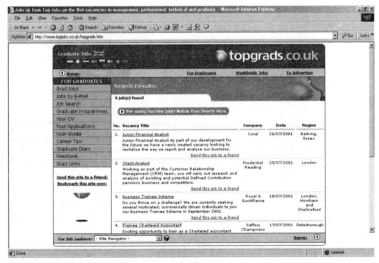

Figure 5.15 New graduate search results

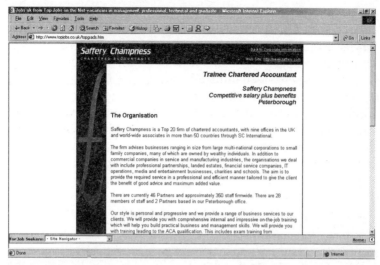

Figure 5.16 Details of the Trainee Chartered Accountant job

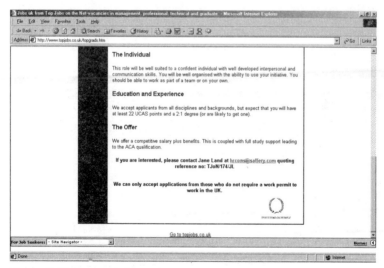

Figure 5.17 Contact information

limited to an e-mail address there is a job number, personal contact and the fact that the e-mail address is the firm's (we know this because the e-mail address ends with @saffery.com).

Now that Jane is comfortable with the fact that this is a legitimate job posting, she needs to respond. To be professional, she must follow instructions and that means responding via the method the company indicates. In this case, she should send an e-mail to Jane Land at the e-mail address hrcons@saffery.com and she should quote reference TJoN/174/JL.

> Want a hint on the purpose of these job or position numbers? Companies and recruiters pay to post positions so they want to track what responses they get from what job boards. From this job number, TJoN/174/JL, you can speculate that TJoN stands for Top Jobs on the Net (the name of the site), 174 probably indicates that this is the 174th position the firm has posted to the Net, and JL means July – the job was posted in July.

So, Jane's found a good job opportunity and needs to respond. Like you, Jane has her electronic CVs and covering letter templates, which she prepared from the advice in Chapters 2 and 3, and she has set up her confidential e-mail as in Chapter 4. So the elements of her job search are just waiting to be put together.

Let's start with the covering letter, as minor adjustments need to be made. Jane developed a number of covering letters during her preparation time but her template for answering job ads, document TextCoverLetter3.txt, is found in her Job Hunt folder. So she needs to open the document (see Figure 5.18).

Once open, Jane needs to change this document from a template to the real thing by filling in the blanks of the template. This includes the addressee, the job title and the job number (see Figure 5.19).

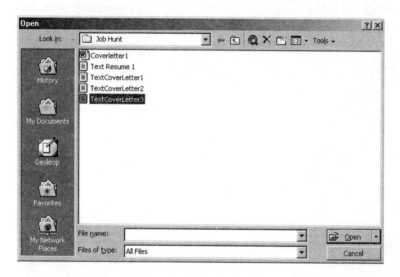

Figure 5.18 Opening a covering letter template

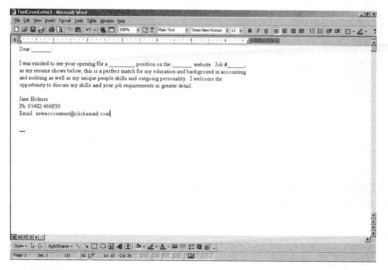

Figure 5.19 The covering letter template

Jane addresses the covering letter to Jane Land, adds the job title of Trainee Chartered Accountant and inserts the job number. If she wants to make any additional changes or do any 'tweaking' to match better the job requirements and keywords from the job posting to the covering letter, now is the time.

The next step is to perform a spell-check and save the document in the Job Hunt folder using a file name that she will recognize as coinciding with this job and this date. A good file name would be SafferyCovLet724.txt. This has the company name and the date so she can quickly refer to the specific covering letter she submitted and when she did so (see Figure 5.20).

All right, the covering letter is ready and so is the CV so it's time to open the e-mail program or go to the site of the free e-mail account. Jane goes to www.clickamail.com and logs in using her user name 'newaccountant' and password 'milo' (see Figure 5.21).

Once successfully logged in, Jane needs to create or compose a new message (see Figure 5.22).

Now it's time to put all the pieces together (see Figure

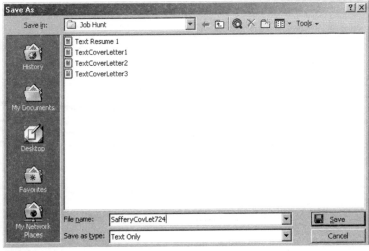

Figure 5.20 Saving the covering letter

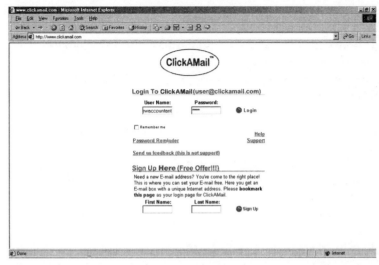

Figure 5.21 Logging in to the e-mail account

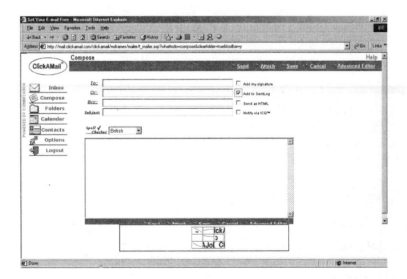

Figure 5.22 Composing a message

5.23). Start by addressing the e-mail message to the addressee. In the 'To:' field of the message, enter the exact e-mail address provided in the e-mail job posting, in this case hrcons@saffery.com. This is incredibly important. Make a mistake here, even by one letter, number or symbol, and your message will never be received and this job opportunity lost for ever. Take the time to double-check it.

Next, enter the subject line. This can be incredibly important, as first impressions are everything. As suggested in Chapter 4, use a strong subject. In this case, Jane could use something like 'Top Accounting Graduate – #TJoN/174/JL'. As Jane is an accountant, adding the job number to the subject line may make her appear more detail- and number-oriented.

The third step is to copy and paste your revised covering letter into the body of the e-mail message. By now you should be an old hand at this; refer back to Chapters 2, 3 or 4 if you need assistance.

You are not done quite yet – you need to add the text CV. Because the job posting did not indicate that attachments were acceptable, you need to paste the CV into the body of the message to be safe. Open your text CV from your Job Hunt folder, and copy and paste it into the body of the e-mail message – below your covering letter (see Figure 5.24).

Now your message, your response to that perfect job posting, is ready to go. Although you've spell-checked it, sent it to 50 friends and know it is perfect... take a deep breath and give it one more review. Remember, you only have one time to make a good first impression. Especially double-check the e-mail address, job title and job number.

What if the company indicates that attachments are acceptable?

In Chapter 4 we discussed how to attach your CV to an e-mail message. All the steps are the same in terms of preparing the e-mail message, adding the subject line and

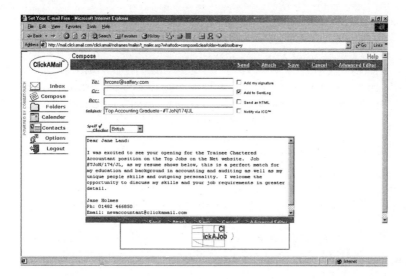

Figure 5.23 Putting the pieces together

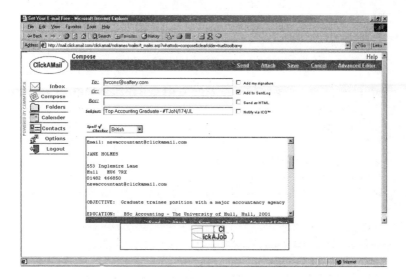

Figure 5.24 Copying and pasting the CV into the e-mail

revising and pasting in your covering letter. However, in addition to pasting your CV into the body of the message – remember, better safe than sorry – also attach it just as you did in Chapter 4. Here are some pointers though:

- Always follow whatever directions the company indicates, ie attachments accepted or not, and covering letter necessary or not.
- If attachments are acceptable and a program or program and version are preferred, eg Microsoft Word 6.0, only attach if you have that specific program and version.
- When in doubt as to whether to attach or not, use common sense, but always paste a text version directly into the body of the e-mail message. Better to send a no-frills version than to have no version read at all.

What if a company wants me to respond directly through a form or link on the job posting?

Many companies are starting to control the process by which job seekers communicate with them, so don't panic – that was the purpose in getting all your covering letters and CVs prepared ahead of time. As companies implement more sophisticated versions of recruiting software, trends will include not only online submission via forms but also pre-employment screening tests for skills and personality. But let's deal with the here and now – the future will be waiting for us.

Figure 5.25 shows an example of a company requesting submission via a form that Jane discovered during her job hunt.

As you can see, the job posting ends with a link to 'Apply Now'. So that's the next step – click on it and see what you need to do (see Figure 5.26).

Although each online form submission will have its own

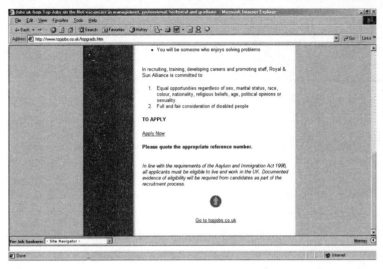

Figure 5.25 Company requesting submission via a form

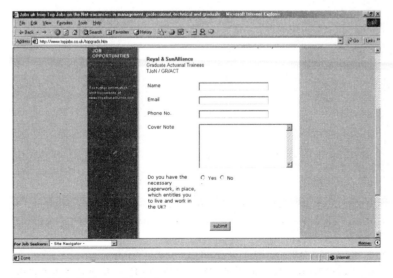

Figure 5.26 Online submission

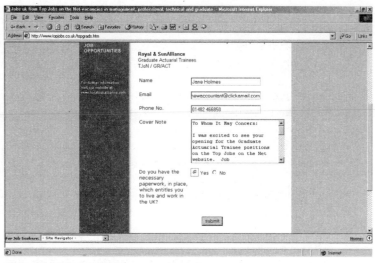

Figure 5.27 Pasting in the covering letter

character, you simply need to follow the instructions. So for this form, Jane needs to fill in the blanks, pasting her revised covering letter (after she has spell-checked it) into the section for cover notes (see Figure 5.27).

Once you click 'submit' and send this first screen through, another screen and set of directions will appear. This particular firm directs you to their Web site and Graduate Career Centre where you can learn more about the firm and its opportunities. Each firm is different, but simply follow the directions and submit the information requested.

Is posting to a CV bank or job board worth it?

There are literally hundreds of CV banks and job boards where you can post your CV free, and yes, it can certainly be worth it. However, just as you take the time to check a job site before you search it and you take the time to review a job posting closely before you apply to it, you have to decide what this CV bank can do for you and where it might let you down in terms of privacy.

There are three types of CV banks you need to be aware of:

- Open. This means anyone can post and anyone can read your CV. No user, either job seeker or recruiter, needs to use a password. These types of CV banks are typically restricted to small local career sites or small associations. There are no major sites that lack at least some control as to who posts CVs and who reads them.
- Password-protected. This means the job site screens employers and recruiters so that only those screened will have a password and access to the CVs. Just like you need a password to register to post your CV to a major job board, an employer or recruiter will need to register and typically pay to view your CV. Most of the majors offer this type of service including TotalJobs (www.totaljobs.com) and Gis-a-Job (www.gis-a-job.com).
- Candidate-controlled databases. This means that the recruiter or employer can only contact you through your CV bank account. A confidential CV (as discussed in Chapter 4, to protect your identity from your current employer) in combination with a candidate-controlled CV bank provides the greatest level of job-search confidentiality. JobPilot (www.jobpilot.co.uk) is a good example of a candidate-controlled CV bank, as employers can only contact you through your CV account on the site.

So, before you post your CV to any site, read the privacy statement. Make sure that your CV and/or contact information are not being sold or provided to any other site or CV bank that may have lesser controls. Likewise, if the site cannot allow you to make changes to or remove your CV at your convenience, this is probably not a site you need to post to. There are simply too many quality sites out there.

A word of caution here: in an effort to keep CV banks fresh for their paying customers (companies pay for access to these banks), CV banks typically purge CVs over 90 days old. So each time you post to a new job bank, make a note of the storage policies so you can re-post if you feel it worth while.

How do you post your CV to a CV bank?

Like everything else you've learnt in this chapter, preparation is the key. If you have the parts assembled, putting them all together is easy. Most CV banks have CV forms, where you fill in the blanks. Be sure to have your CV handy; it's easier and more accurate to cut and paste an existing document than to start from zero every time. Your submission will be more polished (and, therefore, powerful) and there is less chance of spelling mistakes; with the ready availability of spell-checking, typos are a clear sign of sloppiness.

Some of these submission forms will accept text posted from your word-processing program, while others will require an ASCII file. Just yesterday, in the 20th century, sending out 100 CVs was a real chore. Now you can get your CV in front of thousands of employers every time you post a CV.

Each job site is a little different but if you have your tools ready and follow the site's instructions, you should be fine. Here is an example of posting your CV to a job board using the popular site Gis-a-Job (www.gis-a-job.com) (see Figure 5.28).

Right from the front page under the menu choices for job seekers (far left-hand column), the number one option is to register your CV. By clicking on that option, you will go through a very simple process – very similar to e-mailing your CV to an employer.

A nice feature of this particular site is its free and automatic distribution of your CV to all registered recruitment

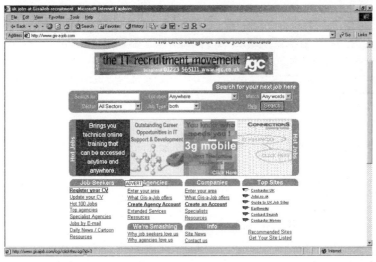

Figure 5.28 Posting your CV to a job board

agencies and companies that post jobs to its job board. (See the sentence directly underneath the logo in Figure 5.29. This means that within 24 hours of posting your CV to this site, you are automatically in front of hundreds of hiring professionals – so you had better put your best foot forward. Don't worry; we have you covered!)

So, here we have a very typical CV posting form. Simply fill out the fields required. Here is an important point of interest though. Some questions may force you to be too specific and cost you job opportunities, so watch your answers. Questions on job location or relocation preferences and salary are big issues. Until you have a sound handle on the job board or unless you are in a position to be very picky, leave your answers broad.

For example, instead of listing the name of the small town you live in, name the area or region of the country – you can always say no to a job opportunity but you can't say yes to something you were never offered. Likewise, be vague about salary – often that is a deciding factor with the company. But again, all things can be negotiated if given the right opportunity or the right person for the job.

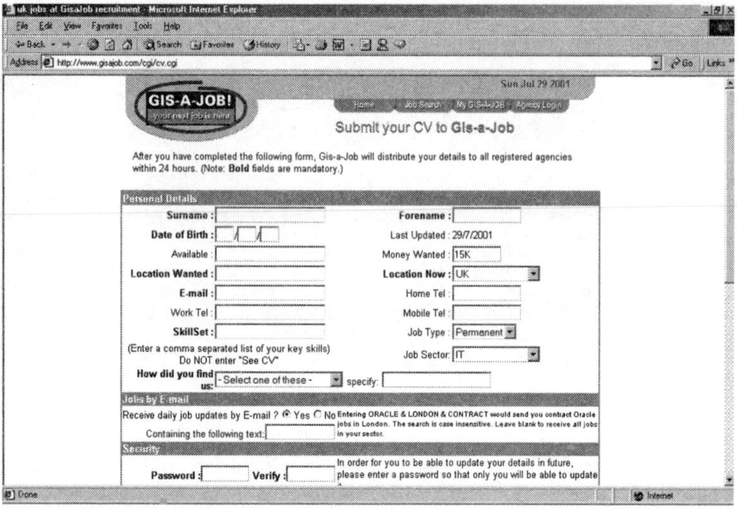

Figure 5.29 Submitting your CV to Gis-a-Job

Jane, our new graduate accountant, would best complete the form as shown in Figures 5.30 and 5.31.

In Figure 5.30, notice first that typically only required fields are completed – in other words, no phone numbers. There is no reason to invite telemarketers even though we have every reason to trust the integrity of the site. Second, both the location (UK) and salary (negotiable) are left very broad. The skill set section is actually an accumulation of all the keywords on Jane's CV.

The bottom half of the CV posting form (see Figure 5.31) includes other notable features.

First, there is a security section that indicates that via the password you choose you have the ability to update or remove your CV at any time. That's a good feature – when you become employed you may have a nervous employer who would take offence at your continued career management. In addition, over time you will gain new skills and, if your CV is still available, you will need the means to update it or risk future employers not having a clear picture of your skills.

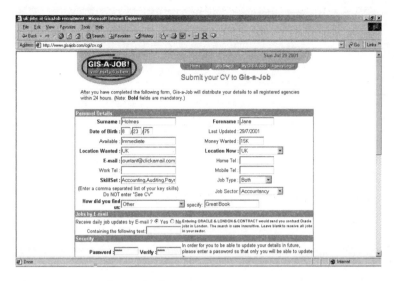

Figure 5.30 Completing the form (1)

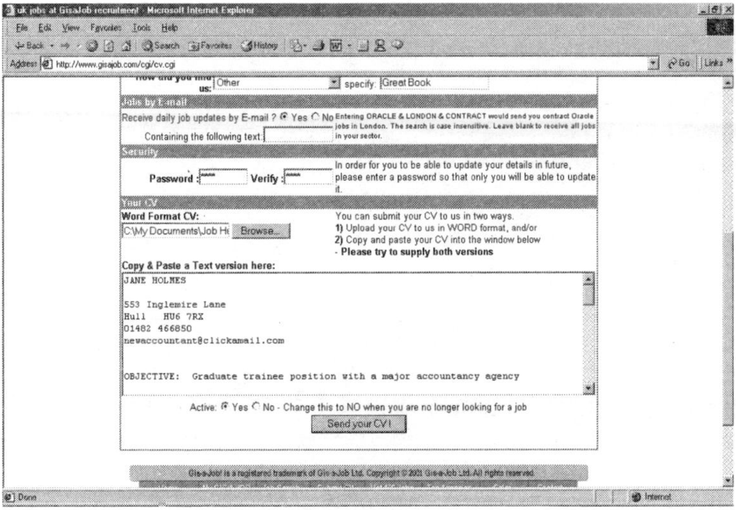

Figure 5.31 Completing the form (2)

This site also allows you the option of posting your CV via a Microsoft Word document or pasting it into a field on the site. As you are knowledgeable in both options, you do both.

Directly above the 'Send your CV!' button is the option to keep your CV active or inactive. This again is a great feature.

One feature we have not yet mentioned is in the centre of the form. It is called 'Jobs by E-mail', and we will get to this time-saving service in a few paragraphs.

Once you've submitted your CV (see Figure 5.32), you want to keep track of your password and take some time to explore all the features these advanced sites offer.

This site, as with many of the majors and large geo-graphic- and functionally specific sites, offers a large array of speciality search profile savers, matching job results storage, industry news updates and, best of all, e-mail job delivery. In essence, why go to search for jobs every week or every day if new matches can be delivered to you?

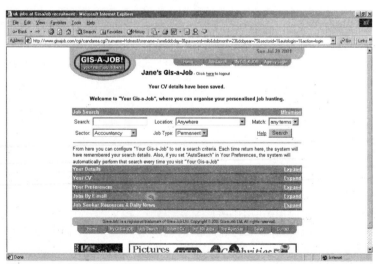

Figure 5.32 Your Gis-a-Job

Do these job delivery services really work?

Many sites are offering delivery of job postings directly to your e-mail address. That's great unless your e-mail box gets stuffed full of jobs that are not for you – just one of the reasons we showed you how to refine your search criteria. Here's how it works: it's called 'push technology'. Essentially the site will take stock of all of its jobs once a day or so. Then, via category and keywords, it organizes this mass of data. When you sign up for the job-delivery service, you'll be asked to complete a questionnaire. Often this is in tandem with a CV posting (as in the previous example) or when you have the option to save your search criteria. This allows the site's software to compare your questionnaire answers to their organized inventory and then 'push' the matching jobs to you.

Here's the problem: if you don't complete the questionnaire carefully, you could get anything from no jobs to far too many jobs. Make sure you can adjust your questionnaire or profile at any time and cancel delivery if you so desire. This push technology can be very helpful and save you time if used properly. Likewise, having the jobs e-mailed to you can help you build a long-time career management database and contact manager for future reference.

Like any good search tool, the better the instructions given to the search engine, the better the matches, so be prepared to change your search criteria until you have them 'tweaked' just right. The sites that offer e-mail job delivery or notification do so in different ways. Some will send you an entire list of new jobs daily or weekly while others will send you a list of links that enable you to click directly to a matching job. Regardless, your job search will certainly increase the amount of e-mail you receive so having separate accounts for work, home and job search will make sense very quickly.

What is this WAP technology I hear about?

WAP stands for Wireless Application Protocol and is a service offered by most of the major job sites, notifying you through your mobile phone or hand-held device of new openings that match your job-search criteria.

Often just a notification or job number is sent to your wireless account telling you to check your regular e-mail account for complete details and links to the actual job postings. You can then access the jobs that have been delivered directly to your personal e-mail account. This is a free service that is readily catching on throughout the major Web sites of the UK. It is advisable to keep an eye out for this feature, as it is cutting-edge.

If I know what company I want to work for, how do I find its Web site and send my CV?

We've spent a great deal of time in this chapter talking about ways to get your CV 'out there'. You've learnt how to respond to job postings you've found on job boards and how to post your CV to CV banks. Believe it or not, there are more aggressive and direct means – go directly to the company.

While the CV banks are a godsend to people on both sides of the desk, company home pages are your very best resource – even though posting to them individually may take a little more time.

The majority of the millions of companies with an Internet presence use part of their site as a recruitment vehicle. It is increasingly probable that those companies you drive by every day on the way to work have a Web site where they post their job openings or at the very least invite the submission of a CV. By delivering directly to the site you will set yourself apart from all the CVs coming in as a result of Internet recruitment advertising.

In addition, company Web sites offer information about the company (histories, press clippings, financial data in the case of public companies) so you can readily customize your covering letter and even your CV.

When you see one of those companies on the way to work (you know, the ones 10 minutes from home instead of an hour), jot the name down and then go on the computer and track down their e-mail address. Finding a company Web site is not a difficult process and you don't need the help of Scotland Yard. Initially try these tricks:

- Type the company name as the URL in your Internet browser (for example, try www.companyname.co.uk – it just might work) or use a search engine. Also try other extension – instead of .co.uk try .com, .net, .org, .org.uk and .ac.uk. Each of these extensions supposedly has meaning but the truth is the Internet grew too fast and no one was paying attention.
- Try this same technique but use variations on the company name, for example include the 'the' or 'company' or 'co' in its name. Just play around with abbreviations, variations and slogans for a couple of minutes in addition to trying the next technique.
- Type the company name into the search engine of your choice such as www.uksearchengine.com, www.mirago.com, and www.uk.yahoo.com.
- Use one of the electronic yellow pages. Most include company information and location maps: www.yell.co.uk, www.londonstockexchange.com or www.askali]x.co.uk, which claims to have the largest Web-based business directory in Europe.

If a company has a Web site, one if not all of these techniques will help you find it. In the next chapter you learn how to take this a step further and identify companies in your industry and area that you never knew existed.

Once on a company's home page, check it out for the following links and information:

- contact information;
- management team biographies;

- career centre and job information;
- a search engine;
- product and service information;
- customer or client information.

These links are the keys to your interview preparation and method for submitting your CV. Always start at the front page – there is a reason it is at the beginning. Earlier in this chapter, UK Siemens (www.siemens.co.uk) was indicated as a good corporate site. Let's take a closer look.

Now, you may have to search around a bit, but most company sites will have a career or job section, and that is where you will discover how to send them your CV. Siemens offers a link to its career centre right at the top centre of the front page (see Figure 5.33).

On clicking on the 'Career Opportunities' link, you are given an option to explore graduate opportunities or professional opportunities (see Figure 5.34).

At many an employer Web site, you may be able to search current openings and submit a formatted CV or an ASCII

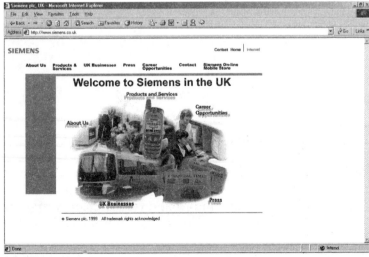

Figure 5.33 Siemans Web site front page

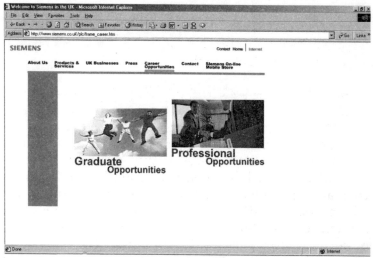

Figure 5.34 Kinds of opportunities available

version, or be required to cut and paste into a CV template designed for the company. Submit it in whatever format they request or you'll risk offending them and your CV being discarded.

In the case of the UK Siemens site, the professional opportunities link leads you to a search engine to search all European Siemens job openings. Let's conduct a search for a mid-level business development professional (see Figure 5.35).

Many opportunities are returned including those shown in Figure 5.36.

Upon choosing the position of interest, a quick click on the job title reveals many more details (see Figure 5.37).

To respond to the job opportunity, all you have to do is click on the 'Apply' button at the bottom of the job posting (see Figure 5.38).

This leads to a CV and information submission form very typical of those most company recruitment sites utilize (see Figure 5.39).

As with any submission form, be careful not to block yourself into a corner regarding questions about relocation

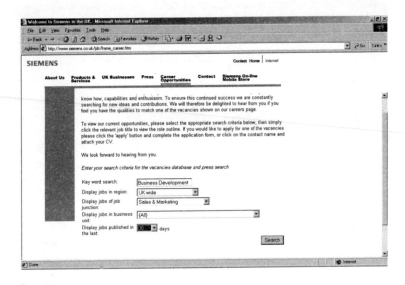

Figure 5.35 A search for a mid-level business development professional

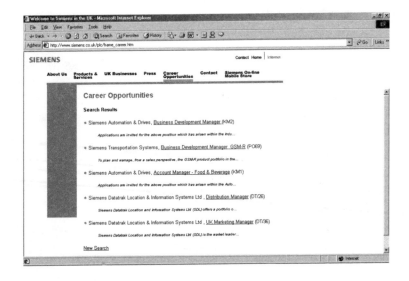

Figure 5.36 Opportunities returned

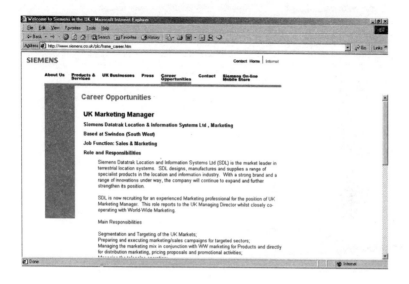

Figure 5.37 Details of the job

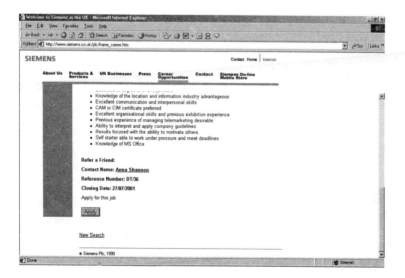

Figure 5.38 Clicking on the 'Apply' button

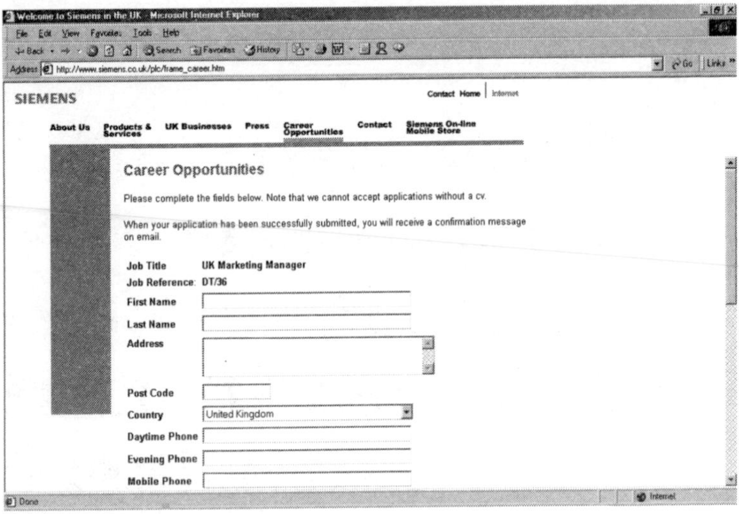

Figure 5.39 CV and information submission form

and salary requirements. As you identify the dream
employers, you should take time to read their job postings
for a while. They will have specific ways of describing their
openings, which you can reflect in a customized CV.

Just as with job banks, company job banks will purge CVs
after so many days (though typically longer than job banks).
So find a policy if you can or keep track of the date you submitted your CV and go back approximately every six months.

Company Web sites offer much more information than
job openings and links or forms to submit a CV. A site like
UK Siemens is great but do not stop your search and explo-
ration at the career centre. Continue to look at other areas
for contact information and management team biographies
most importantly. These are often found through links
called 'about us' and 'contact us'. On company sites that
lack a career centre or HR link, often you can find a specific
contact in your function or an HR executive.

In the next chapter, we will show you how to apply these
techniques to a number of specific search strategies that will
help you customize your online job hunt to your unique
career needs.

six

How should I organize my attack plan for maximum results?

How do I know how many and which sites are best for me?

Now that your job-search tools are ready to go and you've seen what the different types of job boards can do, you need a plan. Even the best football team in the world won't win if it doesn't have a solid strategy.

Your online job-hunting strategy should be in direct correlation with your current job status, level of experience and career goals. For example, maybe you are unemployed and need a job now. Perhaps you are just contemplating a career move, or you have your eye on that company down the street. Likewise, strategies are slightly different for new graduates and senior executives; new graduates simply needn't worry about word getting out about their job search. And always, your strategy must be effective in helping you achieve your prime objective – that special new opportunity.

There are four basic strategies that you can implement throughout different stages in your career. Each utilizes various types of job sites, a different number of job sites and varying degrees of confidentiality. The four strategies are:

- full-scale attack;
- mini attack;
- secret attack;
- mission *not* impossible attack.

Let's take a closer look at each one.

The full-scale attack

The full-scale attack is just as it sounds, a full-blown, no-holds-barred use of every type of site and resource applicable to your level and profession. This attack is best for someone who needs a job right now, someone who is unemployed or newly graduated, who has no time to waste and who needs to get his or her CV into decision makers' hands today. The approach:

- Typically the full-scale attack is used by someone who is unemployed or newly graduated.
- Use *all* of the major and top 10 must-view sites.
- Go to Appendix A and make heavy use of several geographic- and functionally specific sites – at least five to seven of each if possible.
- Join or at least monitor the job sites of two to four associations.
- Post your CV to all of these sites. There is no need for confidentiality so get your CV out there!
- Sign up for job-delivery services and job-posting storage wherever possible.

Here are some special considerations when implementing this strategy:

░ Be prepared for an overwhelming response! Yes, between job delivery, your CV posting and your direct response to adverts, your e-mail box will be over-flowing. So consider using several e-mail accounts and sign up for free accounts on the sites that offer them – this will help you stay organized.

░ When posting your CV, remember that you will be employed soon, so only post to sites that allow you to remove or amend your CV at your convenience. You do not want to make your new employer nervous by keeping your CV out there for all to see.

░ Think long term. The work you are putting into your job hunt today is the foundation for your long-term career management. As the strategies that follow use fewer and more specialized sites, use this strategy as your test base. Keep track of those major sites, geographic- and industry-specific sites so you know which ones gave the best results. These will be the sites that you continue to watch over time.

░ Once you have successfully implemented the full-scale attack strategy you are not done. Career management is a lifetime process and that means you need then to implement the secret attack strategy, which will keep you consistently apprised of all suitable opportunities.

The mini attack

This strategy is a scaled-down version of the full-scale attack. This attack is best for someone who wants to make a change in the near future and most likely is currently employed. It is an approach that may be eminently suitable for someone who is unemployed but is at a professional level where too much exposure is inappropriate:

░ Use 5 to 7 of the major and top 10 sites – choose sites according to the level of confidentiality you need.

░ Use three to five geographic- and industry-specific sites.

- Join and monitor at least two professional associations.
- Post your CV only to those sites that provide the level of confidentiality you require.
- Sign up for job delivery wherever possible including WAP services if you have wireless access.
- Make contact with at least five recruiting and head-hunting firms specializing in your function or industry.

Here are some special considerations when implementing the mini attack:

- Confidentiality is dependent on the employer's support of your job change if employed, or the level or industry if you are unemployed, so choose major job sites and CV posting accordingly.
- Only post your CV to those sites that will allow you to amend or remove your CV at your convenience and support a confidential CV if you need one.
- Just as with the full-scale attack, the effort you put into this job hunt can be worked into the long-term management of your career. So keep track of the sites, associations and recruiters who are most helpful. Likewise, if you are not getting ample results, stop using that site and replace it with another.
- Once you have successfully moved to another position, immediately update your CV postings, make them confidential and implement the secret attack strategy.

The secret attack

This strategy is for someone who is employed but who will move for the right opportunity and therefore just wants to keep an eye on the scene – good career management. This should become part of everyone's long-term career management strategy. Consequently, this strategy should also be used after you have successfully secured a position using any of the other strategies:

- Only two or three of the major or top sites are used.
- Only sites offering job delivery are used – you are employed and your time is too valuable to go to sites and search.
- Your search profile can afford to be far more demanding as you are only interested in really interesting opportunities.
- Only confidential CVs are posted.
- Industry-specific and association use is limited to those two to three sites that offer consistent results and delivery of industry news and events.
- Heavy use of industry- or functionally specific recruiters or headhunters is a must. Contact three to five new firms on a monthly basis. Appendix A lists links to hundreds of recruiting firms to assist you with this, and www.totaljobs.com also has a great database searchable by function.

Some special considerations when using a secret attack include:

- You are currently employed and your confidentiality must be maintained or your job is at risk. Pay special attention to the issues and techniques raised in Chapter 4 on protecting your privacy and online identity.
- Never use your current employer's computer or e-mail account to check or carry out any part of your career management.
- Your time is valuable so utilize job-delivery services offered by the job sites.
- Use professional associations and functional sites to help you stay on top of all the issues relating to your career and your industry in general.
- Headhunters make for valuable friends in long-term career management. They understand your need to be confidential and will come to you when opportunities arise. Try to help headhunters whenever you can, and in return they will help you. A friend or two in the head-hunting business are good friends to have.

The mission not *impossible attack*

This strategy is for the person, employed or unemployed, who has identified the exact company or companies that he or she wants to work for. The essence of this attack is to find a way to get in the door, and there are some easy tricks for you:

- Find the company Web site and do your research. If you don't have the URL, then use directories such as www.yell.co.uk, www.askalix.co.uk or www.london-stockexchange.com.
- In Chapter 5, you learnt how to search a company Web site for the career centre, executive biographies and press releases – do this.
- Send your CV to human resources and key company executives.
- Join professional associations and use the members' directory to look for employees of the company – make professional contact with them, possibly seeking a mentor.
- Sign up for industry newsletter delivery and track the company's actions – stay on top of company growth, new products and clients.
- Even if you are receiving e-mail alerts from these sites, it doesn't hurt to check in on them once a month.
- As even company sites often purge their CV banks, it doesn't hurt to re-send your e-CV a couple of times a year.

Considerations when using the mission *not* impossible attack include:

- Do not be a pest. Always keep your correspondence professional and to the point. Do not contact HR too often – more than every three to six months – as this can be viewed as an annoyance.
- Networking with company employees is the best way

to open the door. Spend your time making contacts through on- and offline associations.

- If you are or have been employed by an industry competitor, be sure to note that in your correspondence with the company.
- Often there is a company in your own backyard that you are not aware of. Use the company search feature of Totaljobs.com (www.totaljobs.com) to search 65,000 companies across geographic and industry criteria – a great tool.

Top 10 must-view sites for any job hunt

While we have identified 1,001 excellent career-oriented sites for you in Appendix A, any first-time online job hunt should begin with visits to each of these top 10 must-view sites.

After extensive research and months of tracking the major job sites of the UK (changing our minds on many of the originals), here is a review and summary of what we believe to be the top 10 must-view sites. Please note these are listed alphabetically, with two US-based sites added at the end because of their strong commitment to creating a UK-specific version of their sites.

ClickAJob

Featured in earlier chapters, ClickAJob (www.clickajob.com) is an HR portal and meta site (ie it has the ability to search other job sites and return results). Its claims to be the 'largest searchable human resources portal in the UK' are very probably true. Without a doubt, the 70,000-plus daily jobs, combined with an amazing number of career links, make it an awesome resource for any job seeker. Owned by the Scandinavian media group Sondagsavisen a-s, ClickAJob offers free e-mail and e-mail job delivery, and very

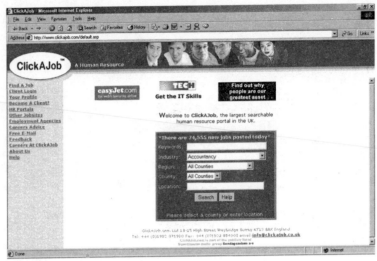

Figure 6.1 ClickAJob

location-specific search engines with hundreds of links to other job sites, career advice and company sites.

Fish4Jobs

Fish4Jobs (www.fish4jobs.com) is just one channel of the Fish4.com family of sites that includes Fish4Cars and Fish4Homes to name a few. Developed by a partnership of nearly 80 per cent of the UK's regional newspaper groups, Fish4Jobs features more than 30,000 jobs daily from these resources. Although there is a high percentage of IT jobs, you are likely to find local jobs here that you wouldn't find on other sites and that makes this site a winner. You can save your job search results in a personal folder and have jobs e-mailed to you, in addition to a nice variety of career advice including links to online courses and psychometric tests.

Figure 6.2 Fish4Jobs

Gis-a-Job

Gis-a-Job (www.gis-a-job.com) claims to be the UK's original, largest, free Web site. Looking at its company

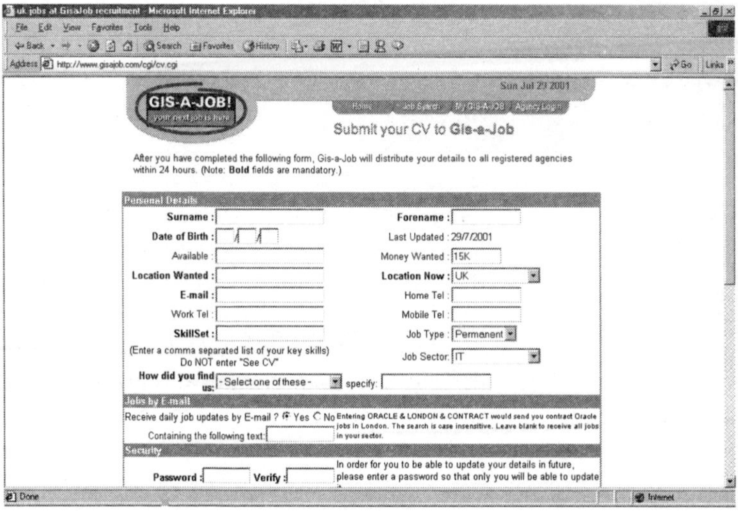

Figure 6.3 Gis-a-Job

history, you'd be hard pressed to disagree. But don't look at this site as a dinosaur. In fact, Gis-a-Job was the first WAP (Wireless Application Protocol – job delivery to your mobile phone or palm device) accessible site. Now that's cutting-edge. Complete with a nice search engine powered by location, categories and keywords, the CV posting service is tops, allowing the job seeker to post via all convenient methods and distributing the CV within 24 hours to all registered agencies free – that's service!

GoJobSite

GoJobSite (www.gojobsite.co.uk) is the longest-established and largest European job site. Its deep relationships with top UK and European organizations and recruiters make it a great site, covering 35 job sectors including IT, telecommunications, sales and marketing, accounting, engineering and administrative to name a few. GoJobSite offers a large array of services that truly assist the job hunter from CV distribution to e-mail delivery of industry news and events in

Figure 6.4 GoJobSite

addition to an efficient search engine that manages over 140,000 job postings. This site requires the job hunter to complete a lengthy registration to utilize its services – it is worth every second invested!

StepStone

StepStone (www.stepstone.co.uk) is another international site that has a great UK presence, featuring more than 100,000 international jobs and averaging around 20,000 in the UK. Job postings are just the tip of the iceberg as far as this site is concerned. As founding members of the Association of Online Recruiters (www.aolr.org), StepStone's commitment to job-hunter privacy and to the quality and timeliness of job information is unmatched. StepStone offers a substantial job search engine featuring 22 categories, CV posting and distribution services, job e-mail delivery including WAP service as well as a large amount of career advice and company profile information. A special service from StepStone is e-mail notification of online

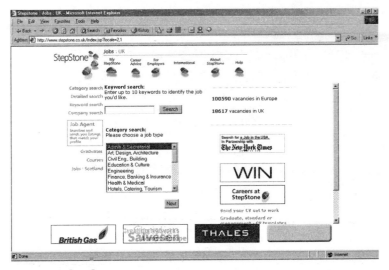

Figure 6.5 StepStone

courses and seminars – once again an example of its commitment to the advancement of your career.

Top Jobs on the Net

Top Jobs on the Net (www.topjobs.co.uk) is an international site that specializes in the MPT (management, professional, technical) recruiting sectors. Featured earlier in this book for its speciality graduate site, Top Jobs makes every attempt to cater to all of its markets. In addition to all the typical job site features with the exception of a CV bank, Top Jobs offers an outstanding amount of company profiles and links to recruitment organizations. The career advice is helpful and changes on a regular basis, with a nice and easy feature that allows you to e-mail a job posting to a friend.

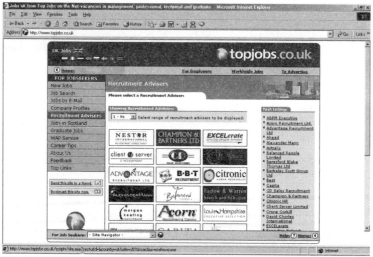

Figure 6.6 Top Jobs on the Net

Totaljobs.com

Totaljobs.com (www.totaljobs.com) offers all the typical features of a major job site with 60,000-plus jobs and some

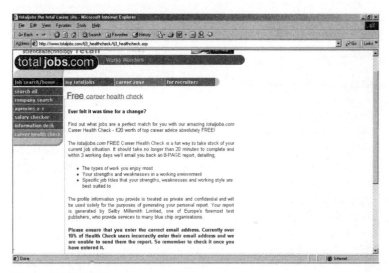

Figure 6.7 Totaljobs.com

truly spectacular 'extras' – take, for example, the search engine that lists how many postings are available in each category. In addition the site features an easy-to-use salary checker, huge database of company profiles, a career doctor and a free career health check-up questionnaire. The site is easy to use and keeps you up to date, including a news service of company workforce changes. This is a real plus. If a company you like is expanding (and who doesn't like an expanding company?), the increase will allow you to approach it even if you haven't run across its job postings yet.

Workthing.com

Owned by Guardian Media Group, Workthing.com (www.workthing.com) appears unique based on its name and appearance alone – but look deeper, as we did. Workthing.com offers searches by several sectors and, once registered, job hunters can use the 'matrix' to save search criteria and see at-a-glance breakdowns of jobs by sector

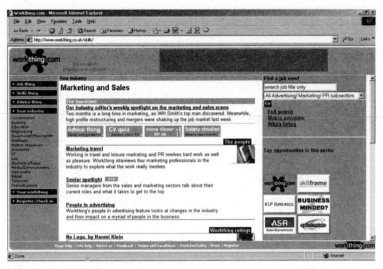

Figure 6.8 Workthing.com

and role. Workthing.com also offers a useful section called 'Skills thing' that helps you find continuing educational resources, links for contract employment and books. 'Your industry' offers 16 areas that feature industry-specific advice, trends and company information. Complete with a salary checker, CV assessment quiz and job e-mail delivery, Workthing.com is a great career site.

In addition to UK- and European-based sites, it would be remiss not to include two US-based sites in the top 10. Both of these sites are rapidly expanding on strong US roots and are entering the UK market full force. With ample experience behind them, look for both of these sites to continue to affect the UK job site and recruitment market.

Monster.co.uk

Monster.co.uk (www.monster.co.uk) really is a monster: more than 30,000 UK jobs, 60,000-plus European jobs and over 1 million jobs worldwide. Monster.com has made a true commitment to becoming the world's premier online

Figure 6.9 Monster.co.uk

recruitment advertising firm and job site. Its attention to detail – to be a true UK site and not a US site painted to look as though it is from the UK – is outstanding. Monster.co.uk has developed a strong infrastructure to assure top job postings, local and relevant career advice, and special communities to assist job hunters from virtually all levels and functional areas.

CareerMosaic-UK/HeadHunter.net

This is a unique situation and deserves to be monitored. CareerMosaic-UK (www.careermosaic-uk.co.uk) has been one of the largest UK job sites over the last two years. Recently, US-based HeadHunter.net purchased CareerMosaic, acquiring both the US and UK sites. At this point, links from CareerMosaic-UK are eventually redirected to HeadHunter.net where there is a small but growing number of UK positions as well as all the typical job-hunter services, career advice and job delivery. As HeadHunter.net gets a handle on its approach to the UK

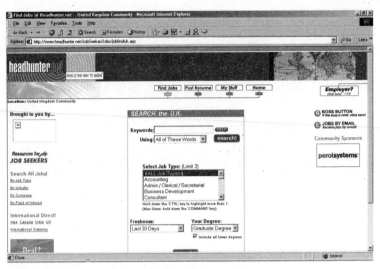

Figure 6.10 CareerMosaic-UK/HeadHunter.net

market, expect to see massive growth on this site, as all the tools and experience are in place from years of experience in the US market where it is extremely well-respected.

seven

I think I'm ready. What am I missing?

You are now better prepared to conduct an online job hunt than 99.9 per cent of the rest of the job-hunting world. With the lack of job security in the modern world of work, this is a skill set you will use time and again throughout your career. If you are employed but looking to move out and up, this is the most comprehensive and time-effective way to do it. You now also have tools and knowledge that will make your smart approach to career management that much easier to administer in the future.

If you are unemployed, right now you have just developed the skills to get not just the first job that comes along and not just any job to get the cash flowing again. This time you will have the opportunity to go out for, and evaluate, every job vacancy available in your field of endeavour.

Have you created a secure online identity?

To conduct a well-organized and professional job hunt you need separate confidential e-mail accounts. These accounts will keep your professional life separate from your personal life. The separation will also keep you focused and keep your job hunt secure and confidential.

Do give some thought to your professional e-mail address; remember that it is a headline that will help get your e-mail communications read. Likewise, pay attention to the subject lines on the e-mails you send, as the subject line is a complementary headline to your e-mail address. If in doubt about a good subject line, you can always use words like 'Top ' or 'Best' followed by the advertised job title.

Is your online CV really ready?

Please do not move forward with your job hunt until your online CV is really ready. You should reread Chapter 2, and then look at your CV afresh and see how it stands up to your scrutiny. Does it describe the professional you succinctly? Have you made an effort to quantify your contributions and achievements wherever possible, in terms of money earned and time and money saved for your employer?

Don't take short cuts on our CV preparation advice. We have not given you superfluous advice to fill up pages, so each of our recommended steps will save you time in the long run and increase your response rate.

Those keywords we have spoken about throughout the book, the verbs and the nouns, are critical to getting your CV read by human eyes. Do make a mental note to jot down keywords from job postings that interest you and include them in your CV wherever applicable to your background. Also check out CVs from people in your field of work whenever you can.

It is difficult to have too many keywords in an electronic CV and they don't all have to be in full sentences. Remember the 'skills' and 'skill set' subheads in the CV examples that allow you to string all these keywords together as a tantalizing appetizer that encourages the reader to get in direct contact with you.

As you build a formatted CV for both online and offline use, be sure that it is scannable and faxable. Evaluate your CV against the scannability checklist in Chapter 2 to ensure that the formatting you have chosen will not confuse the scanning technology.

When you send or fax that hard copy CV you should assume that it will be scanned into a CV database so it must still be scanner-friendly. If you fax your CV you don't want the process to blur the all-important keywords when it comes through someone's fax machine. If you haven't done so yet, be sure to make some practice dry-run mailings to yourself, friends and family, so that you are certain your work is readable on the receiving end.

Finally, check your CV to ensure it is confidential. If you are employed and your employer does not know you are looking, don't give the game away; replace the current employer's name with a generic description such as 'a mid-sized Suffolk food services company' or 'an international financial services conglomerate'. Remove your name and address, being sure to include the contact information of your secure e-mail address in the body of your e-mail covering letter, as well as in the CV.

Do you have covering letter templates prepared?

Your covering letter can be a powerful motivating force, encouraging an employer to get into conversation with you. It is an opportunity to show your organized thought processes. Remember always to apply the three keys to successful covering letter writing:

1. Build a bridge of connectivity between you and the recipient by stating why you are making the contact.
2. Give the recipient a reason to read your CV by stating a link and using some of your keywords. Include at least one sentence about your skill sets and experience. If you work for a direct competitor, say it, as this is a strong plus for your candidacy.
3. Ask for the next step. Say you want to meet and that, if

you don't hear soon, you will take the initiative and make contact.

Are you confident about your ability to identify secure job sites?

Depending on the type of job hunt you will implement, any given site's stance on privacy should be a consideration in your usage of that site. Be sure you do the following:

- Read the site's privacy statement, which is often in small print at the bottom of the home page.
- Favour password-protected sites.
- Only use a site if you can identify who the owners are by name and credentials.
- Be clear about your ability to change, update or remove your CV at any time.
- Don't trust 'blocked' sites to protect your privacy. If the blocking mechanisms fail for any reason, you will be the one whose job could be in jeopardy.
- Never include driving licence number, national insurance number or any professional licence numbers on your CV; these are all doors to your true identity.
- No matter how tempting it is, never use your employer's e-mail to download or send messages at any time during your job hunt.

Have you organized a schedule for your job-hunting day?

Getting a new job is a job in itself, and the harder you work at it the sooner it will be successfully completed. If you are unemployed this should be your sole full-time activity. Dressing as for work in the morning and then getting to your keyboard will help you treat your job hunt as your full-time occupation.

If you are employed you will still be more effective if you give yourself a schedule. This may be a couple of hours in the evening while you set up your confidential attack and then an hour a night as you implement and pursue it. Perhaps it will be a few quiet hours scheduled at weekends. No matter what your strategy is, fixing set times for your activities will get you into the habit and make you much more productive.

Your immediate next steps are to start visiting the recommended sites. Please use Appendix A; we spent considerable time making this a really practical resource. We have visited all of these sites and, based on our considerable experience in the field, we know that they will be of use to you; however, use them intelligently.

Yes, we want you to visit the 10 must-view sites, and we also expect you to visit all the applicable regional sites, which will have jobs the top 10 do not. Appendix A also lists over 700 industry-specific sites – these are huge doors of opportunity for you, and spending the time to visit every one relevant to your profession will be worth it.

You absolutely must visit applicable professional sites, especially the professional association sites. In this instance it is a good idea not only to visit every professional association site for your area of expertise but also to take out membership of at least one of those associations. With association membership you immediately join the inner circle of your profession. If nothing more, you will get a valuable networking directory for your membership dues.

It is better yet if you become actively involved in the association. You will learn about the employment needs of all the members' companies. Through your involvement, this inner circle of professionals will come to know you over time. When a vacancy opens in your field and they are thinking, 'Who do we know?', yours could well be the name that comes to mind. That saying about 'It's not what you know but who you know' does have a grain of truth in it, although we would change it a little to 'It's not just what you know; it's who you made the effort to know that helps.'

At this point you have probably (or nearly) completed your CV as both ASCII text and snappily formatted word-processing documents. While this is a book about online job hunting, it is important that you integrate electronic approaches intelligently with all good job-hunting precepts.

For example, when an especially tasty opportunity comes across your field of vision and you send off your text CV in the body of an e-mail, why not send a traditional, formatted CV too? You hit the employer twice, through different media and with different formats. Given an appealing position with a desirable employer, it is well worth the effort.

The biggest danger to online job hunting is that you are so impressed with the volume of opportunities that you become complacent. We don't want this to happen, because complacency has no role in any well-managed career.

We know that there are industry leaders in any profession, and stellar companies, about which we all say, 'Yes, I'd like to work there.' We want you to start developing a list of these companies. We also want you to take heed as you travel to and from work and in your day-to-day journeys around your area. As you notice interesting and attractive companies, make a note of them and use your online skills to track down their Web sites. Maybe they are advertising for someone like you, and maybe they are not. However, just because a company isn't advertising, or is advertising where you can't see the advertisement, doesn't mean to say it does not have an opening for someone just like you.

Go after specific companies that appeal to you regardless of whether or not you have seen an advertisement. Those companies may have given up on advertising; they may just be about to post an ad; maybe they hired someone who didn't work out and they are quietly looking for a replacement. There are countless reasons why there can be an immediate opening at a particular company, without you knowing about the need. Take control of your life; make a list of highly desirable employers and go about contacting them directly.

In such a case, you can't say in your covering letter that you saw the ad on a job board; instead you might say that, although you haven't seen an advertisement, you find the company a highly desirable employer and want to establish contact to open a dialogue for current and future needs.

Are you prepared for telephone and face-to-face interviews?

Your online activities will generate responses from interested employers, and almost certainly in greater volume than you have ever before experienced. This will result in telephone interviews and face-to-face interviews, followed by second and third interviews and then the offer and negotiation cycle. Given the volume of activity that your online job hunt is likely to generate, you can probably expect to receive more than one offer – assuming of course you know how to handle the interview side of the cycle effectively.

This book is a companion volume to the worldwide perennial best-seller *Great Answers to Tough Interview Questions* (published by Kogan Page), which – if you don't already have it – we strongly recommend you go out and get as soon as possible. It focuses on all the verbal communications that you will engage in during a successful job hunt. In it you will learn what employers are looking for when they make hiring decisions, and you get to see what is behind over 200 difficult or trick questions and how you should answer them to shine in the interview and win the offer. You will find it an invaluable guide to turning your interviews into job offers. It also includes the most comprehensive and practical advice on how best to negotiate job offers to your advantage. You will learn at least as much in the companion volume as you have in these pages. With online job hunting, multiple interviews are in your future. With *Great Answers to Tough Interview Questions* you will learn how to turn those multiple interviews into multiple jobs offers.

Are you aware that smart career management means you are always looking?

Once this job hunt is completed you are fitted to take a far more proactive stance with all your future job hunts. With the skills you have learnt, and the ability to retain everything you do online, you can now keep a permanent eye on the employment scene.

We recommend you maintain your professional e-mail addresses and also your confidential profiles on job banks, and maintain a watchful eye on the employment opportunities that come up in your profession. With all that you have learnt and the 'push' technology of the job banks, in just one or two hours a month you can keep a clear picture of which companies are looking for whom within your profession.

This way your future career steps are likely to be more considered. It is a fact of professional life that if within three years you have not received significant increases and promotions, you have been categorized, stereotyped and pigeon-holed. With a career eye on the Web you can strategize your next step up the ladder well in advance and without the panic that perhaps was attached to this job hunt.

As of right now, you are prepared. You have an outstanding e-CV and covering letter; you have secure professional e-mail addresses. You have a link to every worthwhile career site out there. Plus you have the tools and knowledge for surfing the Internet to find anything and anyone you need to make your next job hunt successful.

We have enjoyed making common sense of something that the experts like to keep mysterious. We told you at the beginning that this wasn't too difficult, and now you know only too well the truth of our claims. There is no more time to waste; take this new-found knowledge and apply it to the enhancement of your career and the quality of your life.

Still got a question? You can reach Terra and Martin at MartinandTerra@careerbrain.com.

The top 1,001 hot UK job sites

During the time that we carried out the formal research on this project, half of what we initially thought of as the top sites merged, were bought, changed their names or simply disappeared into cyberspace. We have visited every one of the sites in this appendix.

While all these top sites are good, you won't have the time, inclination or need to visit them all. You will want to visit a number of sites in each of the 12 categories as they are relevant to your profession, location, level of expertise and the unique needs of your particular job hunt.

Let's start with an overview of each of the 12 categories within this appendix, which will give you a comprehensive understanding of the different types of Web sites that exist to help you in your job hunt:

1. **Top job sites**. These are the biggest and most comprehensive sites out there at présent. Each is home to some great products and services, job banks and CV banks. These sites are a good place to start your online job hunt; spending 20 minutes on each of these sites will not only be educational and helpful to your job hunt, but it will give you a frame of reference by which to evaluate the other specialist sites you will visit. You may find

yourself coming back to these sites; you may discover other sites and site categories far more valuable to you.

2. **Meta job sites**. These are directories or guide sites that list many others sites or have search engines capable of searching many sites at the same time. The types of jobs within the sites that the meta site searches vary from general to government appointments. These are good starting places to get your feet wet and see the huge scope and job offerings available through an online job search. You use a meta site to search for a particular job title and geographic restriction across many sites simultaneously. You must be aware that the meta search engine is a very general one and does not search the Web in its entirety, but only the specific sites it indicates and not specifically using each site's own search engine. This means that the results are general. So, the best advice here is to use the meta search engines to find some sites or job boards that you should then visit directly.

3. **Multi-sector sites**. These sites feature three or more different industry sectors or types of jobs – not quite generalist sites but not absolutely industry-specific either. Often these sites cater to a certain level of professional, like entry-level or executive.

4. **Newspapers and publications**. This category consists mainly of the online presence of newspapers, mirroring the print recruitment advertising from their publications. It includes major newspapers, as well as links to smaller papers, magazines and guides.

5. **Geographic location-specific**. Some sites are geographically based, and some are functional-specific (say banking, for example) and then you can narrow your search by geographic area. Other sites in this section connect to geographic job directories – a good example for this section is UK Village at www.ukvillage.co.uk. This selection is just a start – there are so many more. Note that a good way to find local job boards is to use the search techniques offered in Appendix C.

6. **Graduates**. All of these sites are either dedicated to jobs

for new graduates or have a major portion devoted to the new graduate job market. Many colleges and universities post opportunities directly on their own sites so it is always advisable to go to university home pages. One tool to find the home pages of many colleges is to use a UK Directory such as www.careersportal.co.uk.

7. **Industry- or profession-specific**. This section is broken down further into industry-specific subsections. Each subsection features industry-specific sites that are typically much smaller in nature than the majors, but many companies and recruiters prefer these smaller sites to look for candidates. They may get fewer responses, but the responses they do get are felt to be of a higher calibre. This is important information for the online job hunter, and makes sites in this section especially worthy of your attention. Responding online gives you a plus to begin with; responding online through a specialist site where the recruiters already expect a high-calibre response means that your high-calibre CV can get special attention. Apart from networking, these specialist sites are also valuable for long-term career management, as they allow you to stay connected with your profession and the people within it. Specialist fields include:
   - accountancy, banking and finance;
   - agriculture, fishing and forestry;
   - architecture and construction;
   - art, design and media;
   - consultancy;
   - education and training;
   - engineering;
   - health and social services;
   - information technology;
   - legal;
   - manufacturing, production and procurement;
   - miscellaneous;
   - public sector and charity;
   - retail and wholesale;
   - sales, marketing and advertising;

- science;
- telecommunications;
- transport, logistics and aerospace;
- travel and hospitality.

8. **Diversity**. There is a good selection of sites for those with disabilities, minority groups, women, gays and lesbians, older workers and a variety of nationalities. If you are part of a minority group, job hunting can be a special challenge. You will find these sites supportive and educational. When a company is reaching out to these communities via recruitment advertising, you absolutely want to know about it, as your minority status can suddenly give you an edge.

9. **Corporate links**. Instead of listing specific corporate job pages, we decided, as there are so many, to give you the sites that will help you find any specific company or type of company. We assembled a collection of sites that have information and links to a large number of companies.

10. **Associations**. Most have job listings and links to other organizations or sites of interest to people in that particular field. (A couple of nice sites are ACCA at www.acca.org.uk and ICE at www.ice.org.uk.)

11. **Recruiters, appointment agencies and headhunters**. This collection offers a wide variety of permanent and temporary placement firms, industry-specific firms, some international firms and some firms just for executives. Often these types of sites encourage job seekers to register (put their CV in the database) rather than post actual job openings. Although we have listed dozens of sites, there are many more.

12. **Miscellaneous**. This is an assortment of sites that just didn't fit in anywhere else, but which we feel have something important from the job hunter's point of view. These aren't job bank or CV bank sites. Rather, you will find sites with great information on CV writing, or that feature career and personality tests or that are fun sites offering advice on how to quit your job (eg I-Resign.com and Dumb Bosses).

If you are unhappy in your career, or you are frustrated because you just can't seem to keep a job for very long, you may want to check out some of the personality and career choice tests, and re-evaluate your direction.

The following pages contain 1,001 sites divided among these 12 categories. How you use the pages is up to you and your specific needs. With these site links, the online job-hunting world is your oyster.

1. Top job sites

Click A Job	www.clickajob.com
Gis-a-Job	www.gis-a-job.com
JobSite	www.gojobsite.co.uk
JobPilot	www.jobpilot.co.uk
Monster	www.monster.co.uk
Fish4.com – Jobs	www.fish4.co.uk/jobs/
Reed	www.reed.co.uk
StepStone	www.stepstone.co.uk
Top Jobs	www.topjobs.co.uk
Totaljobs	www.totaljobs.com
Workthing.com	www.workthing.com

2. Meta jb sites

alljobsuk.com	www.alljobsuk.com
ChangeJobs at BTInternet	www.btinternet.com
Careers Portal	www.careersportal.co.uk
GIS Employment Service	www.employmentservice.gov.uk
Employment Backbone	www.iesolutions.net/ backbone.htm
Jobs.co.uk	www.jobs.co.uk
Britain's Job Agent	www.jobs-in-the-uk.com/
UK JobsGuide	www.ukjobsguide.co.uk

3. Multi-sector sites

9 till 5	www.9till5.com
Add Jobs	www.addjobs.co.uk

Career Information and Guidance on the Web	www.aiuto.net/uk1.htm
Career Globe UK	www.careerglobe.co.uk
CareerGlobe	www.careerglobe.com
CareerGuide	www.careerguide.net
Career Mosaic-UK	www.careermosaic-uk.co.uk
Careerplus.com	www.careerplus.com
Career World	www.careerworld.net
Careerzone UK	www.careerzone-uk.com
City Jobs	www.cityjobs.co.uk
CV Index	www.cvindex.com
CVServices.net	www.cvservices.net
datum europe	www.datumeurope.com
Daily Mail and General Trust	www.dmgtopportunities.com
DoctorJob	www.doctorjob.co.uk
eLance	www.elance.com
Execs on the Net	www.eotn.co.uk
EURES	www.europe.eu.int/jobs/eures
Exclusive Careers	www.exclusivecareers.co.uk
Executives on the Web	www.executivesontheweb.com
First Division Jobs	www.firstdivisionjobs.com
First Division People	www.first-divisionpeople.uk.com
Goldjobs.com	www.goldjobs.com
InterviewMe	www.interviewme.co.uk
Job2Job	www.job2job.co.uk
Job Ads	www.jobads.co.uk
Jobbies.com	www.jobbies.com
The Job Channel	www.jobchannel.tv
Job Horizon	www.jobhorizon.com
Job Hunter	www.jobhunter.co.uk
JobLine500	www.jobline500.co.uk
JobMagic	www.jobmagic.net
Job-Market	www.job-market.com
jobmatch.com	www.jobmatch.com
Fish4jobs (formerly JobHunter and others)	www.fish4.co.uk/jobs/
Merseyworld	www.jobs.merseyworkplace.com
jobs.net	www.jobs.net
Jobs-at.co.uk	www.jobs-at.co.uk
Job Scout	www.jobscout.co.uk
Jobs Directory	www.jobsdirectory.co.uk
Job Search	www.jobsearch.co.uk
Jobserve	www.jobserve.co.uk

Job Shark	www.jobshark.co.uk
JobsinWales.com	www.jobsinwales.com
JobSite UK	www.jobsite.co.uk
Jobs Unlimited	www.jobsunlimited.co.uk
Job Track Online	www.jobtrack.co.uk
JobWeb	www.jobweb.com
London Careers	www.londoncareers.net
loot.com – Jobs	www.loot.com
lycos.co.uk	www.lycos.co.uk
Makoot	www.makoot.co.uk
MyCVonline	www.mycvonline.co.uk
Jobs Bulletin Board UK	www.neptune.unet.com
New Monday	www.newmonday.co.uk
nixers.com	www.nixers.com
Onlinecareers	www.onlinecareers.co.uk
Openjumbo.com	www.openjumbo.com
Pathfinder	www.pathfinder-one.com
Phoneajob	www.phoneajob.com
PlusJobsUK	www.uk.plusjobs.com
QuantumJobs.com	www.quantumjobs.com
Qworx	www.qworx.com
RecruitmentScotland	www.recruitmentscotland.com
Reed.co.uk	www.reed.co.uk
Working Mole	www.redmole.co.uk
s1jobs.com	www.s1jobs.com
scotstaff.com	www.scotstaff.com
Search	www.search.co.uk
SelectJob	www.select-a-job.co.uk
SkillsGroup	www.skillsgroup.ie
Step2Work	www.step2work.com
SwiftWork.com	www.swiftwork.com
The Best Jobs	www.thebestjobs.co.uk
TheJob.com	www.thejob.com
The Site	www.thesite.org.uk
Directory of Job Sites	www.transdata-inter.co.uk/jobs-agencies/
TV Jobshop	www.tvjobshop.com
Yahoo Careers UK	www.uk.careers.yahoo.com
ukjobs.com	www.ukjobs.com
UKjobs-Careerzone	www.ukjobs-careerzone.com
vacancies.co.uk	www.vacancies.co.uk
WiltshireJobs.com	www.wiltshirejobs.com
Worktrain	www.worktrain.gov.uk

4. Newspapers and publications

AlljobsUK	www.alljobsuk.com
Newspapers and Trade Magazine Listings	www.alljobsuk.com/ publications.shtml
The Telegraph: Appointments-plus	www.appointments-plus.com
Big Blue Dog	www.bigbluedog.com
The Standard Europe	www.europe.thestandard.com
Guardian Unlimited Jobs	www.jobs.guardian.co.uk
jobsnetwork.co.uk	www.jobsnetwork.co.uk
myOyster	www.myOyster.com
The Missing Link	www.newspapersoc.org.uk/ missinglink/
Peoplebank – Daily Mail Careerlink	www.peoplebank.com/pbank/ owa/careerlink.homepage
A Career in Magazines	www.ppa.co.uk
The Times Appointments	www.revolver.com
Sunday Times Appointments	www.sunday-times.co.uk/ appointments
Supply Management Online	www.supplymanagement.co.uk
The Times Appointments	www.thetimes.co.uk/ appointments
ThisIsYourCareer	www.thisisyourcareer.co.uk
Guardian Unlimited	www.work.guardian.co.uk

5. Geographic location-specific

Hertfordshire – St Albans Guide	http://www.st-albans-guide.co.uk/
Accountancy Options	www.accountancy-jobs-surrey.co.uk
Cambridge Evening News Jobfinder	www.cambridge-news.co.uk/ jobfinder/
Careers Bradford	www.careersb.co.uk
Plan IT	www.ceg.org.uk/planit/
CheshireWorkplace	www.cheshireworkplace.com
Cumbria Careers	www.cumbriacareers.co.uk/
Cumbria Workplace	www.cumbriaworkplace.com
EuroLondon	www.eurolondon.co.uk
Highlands Career Services	www.highlandcs.demon.co.uk
Total Wales	www.icWales.co.uk

Interactive Towns and Cities	www.interactivecities.net
JobM8.com	www.jobM8.com
Jobsearch-today	www.jobsearch-today.com
Job Watch	www.jobwatch.co.uk
Labourmarket.org	www.labourmarket.org/
Lancashire Workplace	www.lancashireworkplace.com
London Jobs Guide	www.londonjobsguide.co.uk
Manchester Workplace	www.manchesterworkplace.com
Mersey Workplace	www.merseyworkplace.com
Modern Apprenticeships	www.modernapprenticeships.co.uk
Scottish Appointments	www.monsterscotland.co.uk
My Village Network	www.myvillage.com
NI Jobs	www.nijobs.com
Northwest Workplace	www.northwestworkplace.com
Opportunity Links	www.opportunity-links.org.uk/
Professional Appointments	www.pro-app.co.uk
Recruitment Ireland	www.recruitment-ireland.com
Recruitment-Online	www.recruitment-online.com
Recruit Northern Ireland	www.recruitni.com
Routeways	www.routeways.com
Shetland Career Services	www.shetland-careers.org.uk
Graduate Link Staffordshire	www.staffsgradlink.co.uk
Teachers4London	www.teachers4london.com
UK Villages	www.ukvillages.co.uk
Workfinder	www.workfinder.co.uk
YorkJobs	www.yorkjobs.co.uk

6. Graduates

1st Job	www.1stjob.co.uk
ActivateCareers	www.activatecareers.co.uk
Best Appointments	www.bestappointments.co.uk
BioMedNet	www.biomednet.com
Career Fever	www.careerfever.co.uk
NorthEast Appointments	www.careers.ncl.ac.uk/ northeastappointments
Prosper Wales	www.cchp2.swan.ac.uk
Capital Markets Consulting	www.cmcx.com
EMDS Recruitment	www.emdsnet.com
Eurograd	www.eurograduate.com
Evolution	www.evolution-tsa.co.uk
Fledglings	www.fledglings.net

GET	www.get.hobson.com
Give me a job	www.givemeajob.co.uk
Graduate Appointments	www.gradapps.co.uk
GraduateBase	www.graduatebase.com
Graduate Jobs in Wales	www.graduate-jobs-in-wales.ac.uk
GraduateLink.com	www.graduatelink.com
Graduate Recruitment Company	www.graduate-recruitment.co.uk
Graduate Recruitment in IT	www.graduates-in-it.co.uk
Gradunet	www.gradunet.co.uk
Gradunet	www.gradunet.com
Graduate Recruitment Bureau	www.grb.uk.com
Growth Graduates	www.growthgraduates.com
GTI Careerscape	www.gti.co.uk
101 Graduate Vocations	www.gti.co.uk/vocations/
Huntahead	www.huntahead.com
Inside Careers	www.insidecareers.co.uk
International Graduate Recruitment: Hobsons	www.intemployment.hobson.com
jobs4grads	www.jobs4grads.co.uk
Media Contacts	www.media-contacts.co.uk
Meta-Morphose Limited	www.meta-morphose.com
Graduate Milkround	www.milkround.co.uk
National Association of Managers of Student Services	www.namss.org.uk/workexp/
Old Skool Network	www.oldskoolnetwork.com
Daedal International	www.ozemail.com.au
Pareto Law PLC	www.paretolaw.co.uk
PhD Recruitment	www.phd-recruitment.com
PlanetGraduate	www.planetgraduate.com
Graduate Link	www.portland.shef.ac.uk/gradlink/
Prospects Web	www.prospects.csu.ac.uk
Graduate Services UK	www.recruitgrads.co.uk
Student123	www.student123.com
The Student Law Centre	www.studentlaw.com
Student Pages	www.studentpages.com
Top Grads on the Net	www.topgrads.co.uk
UK Placements	www.ukplacements.com
Work Experience Bank	www.workbank.man.ac.uk
Wotson.net	www.wotson.net/jobs/graduates/
Year in Industry	www.yini.org.uk

7. Industry- or profession-specific

Accountancy, banking and finance

3sectorjobs.com	www.3sectorjobs.com
accountancy.jobserve.com	www.accountancy.jobserve.com
Solutions Highway – AccountancyPersonnel	www.accountancypersonnel.co.uk
Accounting Technician	www.accountingtechnician.co.uk
accountingweb.co.uk site/jobs.cgi	www.accountingweb.co.uk/cgi-
Arthur Andersen	www.arthurandersen.com
Astbury Marsden Search and Selection	www.astburymarsden.co.uk
Bean Counter Jobs	www.beancounterjobs.co.uk
Capital One	www.capitalone.co.uk/careers/
CIPFA	www.cipfa.org.uk
Cityexec.com	www.cityexec.com
CityHotDesk	www.cityhotdesk.co.uk
Datek Online	www.datek.com/marketing/ career/
Deloitte	www.deloitte.co.uk
doublecuff.com	www.doublecuff.com
eFinancialCareers	www.efinancialnews.com
ErnstYoung	www.ernstyoung.co.uk
Financial Careers	www.financial-careers.co.uk
FinCareers	www.fincareers.co.uk
CareerPoint at FT.com	www.ftcareerpoint.ft.com/ ftcareerpoint
GAAP Web	www.gaapweb.co.uk
Hacker Young	www.hackeryoung.co.uk
Halifax	www.halifax.co.uk/jobs/
High Flyers	www.high-flyers.co.uk
HSBC	www.hsbc.co.uk
Inside Careers – Chartered Accountants	www.insidecareers.co.uk/ accountants/index.htm
Inside Careers – Tax Advisers	www.insidecareers.co.uk/tax/ index.htm
jobsfinancial.com	www.job.co.uk
Jobsfinancial.com	www.jobsfinancial.com
Jobs in Accountancy	www.jobsin.co.uk/accountancy/
Jobs in Banking	www.jobsin.co.uk/banking/
Jobs in Finance	www.jobsin.co.uk/finance/

KPMG	www.kpmgcareers.co.uk
Nat West Group	www.natwestgroup.com
Onvocation.com	www.onvocation.com
PFA	www.pfa.co.uk/pfa-links.htm
PKF	www.pkf.co.uk
Global PriceWaterhouseCoopers	www.pwcglobal.co.uk
recruit-u.co.uk	www.recruit-u.co.uk
The Big Trip	www.thebigtrip.co.uk
City People	www2.citipeople.com

Agriculture, fishing and forestry

Earthworks	www.earthworks-jobs.com
Farming Online	www.farmline.com
Forest Industries Development Council	www.fidc.org.uk/jobs/
Global Association of Online Foresters	www.foresters.org/jobs.html
Forest People International	www.forestpeople.com
Jobs in Agriculture	www.jobsin.co.uk/agriculture/
Jobs in Forestry	www.jobsin.co.uk/forestry/
Jobs in Veterinary	www.jobsin.co.uk/veterinary/
Sea-Ex	www.sea-ex.com/employment/
TimberWeb	www.timberweb.com/jobs/

Architecture and construction

AndersElite	www.anderselite.com
Architects Online	www.architects-online.org
Building Information Warehouse	www.biw.co.uk/
Careers in Construction	www.careersinconstruction.com
Constructioncv.co.uk	www.constructioncv.co.uk
Contract Construction Services Scotland Ltd	www.contractscotland.co.uk
e-Architect	www.e-architect.com
Engineers Site	www.engineerssite.com
Folio Personnel	www.foliopersonnel.com
Jobs in Construction	www.jobsin.co.uk/construction/
Jobs in Surveying	www.jobsin.co.uk/surveying/
Jobs in Architecture	www.jobsinarchitecture.co.uk
Prisma Recruitment Ltd	www.prisma-recruitment.com

Locri Environmental Recruitment   www.sparks.co.uk/locri/
Walbrook Architectural
   Appointments   www.walbrook.net
Workstream   www.workstream.com

Art, design and media

a-n   www.anweb.co.uk
The BBC World of Opportunity   www.bbc.co.uk/jobs/
Applause   www.cnvi.com/applause/
Datascope Recruitment   www.datascope.co.uk/
Design Jobs   www.designjobs.com
Jobs.compelreach.co.uk   www.jobs.compelreach.co.uk
Jobs in Films   www.jobsin.co.uk/films/
Jobs in Media   www.jobsin.co.uk/media/
Jobs in TV   www.jobsin.co.uk/TV/
Journalism.co.uk   www.journalism.co.uk
Media Central   www.mediacentral.net
Media Contacts   www.media-contacts.co.uk
Mousetrapmedia   www.mousetrapmedia.co.uk
Music Directory   www.music-media.co.uk
NewMedia Staff   www.newmediastaff.co.uk
Opportunities Online   www.opps.co.uk
Price Jamieson   www.pricejam.com
Print Job Search   www.printjobsearch.co.uk
productionbase.co.uk   www.productionbase.co.uk
Projector Films   www.projector.demon.co.uk
RecruitMedia   www.recruitmedia.co.uk
SourceThatJob   www.sourcethatjob.com
The SportsWeb   www.thesportsweb.net
The Stage   www.thestage.co.uk
Media Network   www.tmn.co.uk
TS2K Careers In Creativity   www.ts2k.org.uk
Web Job Shop   www.webjobshop.co.uk

Consultancy

Andersen Consulting   www.ac.com/careers/
AT Kearney   www.atkearney.com
ConsultancyJobs   www.consultancyjobs.com
Contractor UK   www.contractoruk.co.uk

Cambridge Technology Partners	www.ctp.com/job/
Customer Systems	www.customersystems.com
Sybase UK	www.freedomatsybase.com
French Thornton	www.french-thornton.co.uk
Inside Careers – Management Consultants	www.insidecareers.co.uk/man/index.htm
Inter Point	www.inter-point.com
PA Consulting	www.pa-consulting.co.uk/careers/
McKinsey Consultants	www.recruiting.mckinsey.com
Syntegra	www.syntegra.com
Top-consultant.com	www.top-consultant.com
Twinserve	www.twinserve.co.uk
WS Atkins	www.wsatkins.co.uk/recruitment/

Education and training

Appointments for Teachers	www.aft.co.uk
Capstan Teachers	www.capstan.co.uk
CareerSoft	www.careersoft.co.uk
DownYourStreet.co.uk	www.downyourstreet.co.uk
Education-Jobs UK	www.education-jobs.co.uk
eTeach.com	www.eteach.com
jobs.ac.uk	www.jobs.ac.uk
Jobs Edufind	www.jobs.edufind.com
Times Higher Education Supplement	www.jobs.thes.co.uk
Jobs in Education	www.jobsin.co.uk/education/
Jobs in Further Education	www.jobsinfe.co.uk
NATFHE	www.natfhe.org.uk
Higher Education Jobs Noticeboard	www.niss.ac.uk/noticeboard/
PhD Jobs	www.phdjobs.com
SchoolsNet	www.schoolsnet.com
Teachers Insite	www.teachers-insite.ie
Teachers Job Search	www.teachersjobsearch.co.uk
TEFL.com	www.tefl.com
Times Educational Supplement	www.tes.co.uk
TES onlinejobs	www.tesjobs.co.uk
The Teacher Net	www.theteachernet.co.uk
Time Plan	www.timeplan.com
UK Teacher Net	www.ukteachernet.co.uk

Engineering

Jobs in Engineering	http://www.jobsin.co.uk/engineering/jobseeker.htm
Engineering Connections	www.apprentices.co.uk
Cadence	www.cadence.com
Celestica	www.celestica.com
e4jobnet.com	www.e4jobnet.com
E for engineers	www.eforengineer.co.uk
Engineers	www.engineers.org.uk
The Engineering Technology Site	www.engineers4engineers.co.uk
Engineers Online	www.engineers-online.co.uk
Engineers on the Net	www.engineersonnet.com
EngineerTalk	www.engineertalk.com
FisitaJobs.com	www.fisitajobs.com
IC-Resources	www.ic-resources.co.uk/asic_index_jobs.htm
Inside Careers – Engineering	www.insidecareers.co.uk/engineering/
Job Shop	www.jobshop.com
Just Engineers.net	www.justengineers.net
The Electronics Contractor's Friend	www.ndirect.com/sorwin/contract.html
Roadwhore	www.roadwhore.com
ShorTerm Engineers	www.shorterm.co.uk
TechCareers	www.techcareers.co.uk
Techistaff	www.techistaff.co.uk
technistaff.com	www.techistaff.com
The Career Engineer	www.thecareerengineer.com

Health and social services

Nursing Web sites	www.british-nursing.co.uk
BUPA	www.bupa.co.uk
Dental Recruitment Online	www.derweb.co.uk/jobs/
The Social Service Research Grapevine	www.grapevine.bris.ac.uk
Health Courses and Careers Update Online	www.healthcourses.co.uk
Health Professionals	www.healthprofessionals.co.uk
Health Service Journal	www.hsj.co.uk
InPharm	www.inpharm.com

JobPharm — www.jobpharm.com/ frameset.html

Jobs in Care Support — www.jobsin.co.uk/caresupport/
Jobs in Health — www.jobsin.co.uk/health/
Jobs in Nursing — www.jobsin.co.uk/nursing/
Medical Hound Dog — www.medicalhounddog.com
MedJobsUK.com — www.medjobsuk.com
NHS Jobs — www.nhsjobs.com
Nursing Practitioners Central — www.nurse.net
Nurse Bank — www.nursebank.co.uk
Nurserve.co.uk — www.nurserve.co.uk
Nursing City — www.nursing-city.com/uk.html
British Nursing Agencies — www.nursing-list.com
Nursing Standards Online — www.nursing-standards.co.uk
Opportunities Online — www.opps.co.uk
Locum Group — www.principal-scientists.co.uk
Radjobs.com — www.radjobs.co.uk

Information technology

1st Choice Computer Appointments — www.1stchoice-itjobs.co.uk
3Sectorjobs — www.3sectorjobs.com
4Weeks.com — www.4weeks.com
ADA People — www.adapeople.co.uk
Aquent — www.aquent.com
Bearpark Jobs Online — www.bearpark.co.uk
Computer Services Corporation — www.careers.csc.com
Certify Now! — www.certifynow.co.uk
Citi Elite — www.citielite.co.uk
Citrix — www.citrix.co.uk/employment/
Compro — www.compro.demon.co.uk
ComputerJobs — www.computerjobs.com
Computer Weekly — www.computerweekly.co.uk
ContractorUK — www.contractoruk.co.uk
Corporate Skills Ltd — www.corporateskills.com
ComputerWeekly — www.cw360.com
Data General — www.dg.com/careers/
Tech Careers — www.dotelectronic.co.uk
DotJobs — www.dotjobs.co.uk
ejob Net — www.ejob.net
EMC — www.emc.com/hr/
FreelanceInformer.com — www.freelanceinformer.com

Inside Careers – IT	www.insidecareers.co.uk/it/index.htm
Intel	www.intel.com
IT Connections	www.itconnections.co.uk
IT Executive	www.it-executive.com
IT JobBank	www.it-jobbank.co.uk
IT JobChange	www.itjobchange.co.uk
it-jobs.com	www.it-jobs.com
ITJobs4	www.itjobs4.com
IT Opportunities	www.it-opportunities.co.uk
IT Pages	www.it-pages.co.uk
JobBoard.IT	www.jobboard.it
jobforce	www.jobforce.co.uk
Jobs Domain	www.jobsdomain.co.uk
JobServe	www.jobserve.com
Jobs in it	www.jobsin.co.uk/it/
JobWorld	www.jobworld.co.uk
Logica	www.logica.com/jobs/
Lucent	www.lucent.com
Madge Networks	www.madge.com
Perfectfit	www.perfectfit.co.uk
Polygons.co.uk	www.polygons.co.uk
ProactivePeople	www.proactivepeople.com
Reflex	www.reflexgroup.co.uk
reviewjobs	www.review.co.uk
Rexonline	www.rex.co.uk
RITS Consultants	www.rits.com
Taps	www.taps.co.uk
Techies.com	www.techie.com
Technojobs	www.technojobs.co.uk
European Job Portal	www.the-job-portal.com
The WorkSite.com	www.theworksite.com
Top Contracts	www.topcontracts.com
Virtual Job Finder	www.virtualjobfinder.com
WorkingPlaces.com	www.workingplaces.com
zzJobs	www.zzjobs.com

Legal

Bloomer McCrum Legal Recruitment	www.bloomermccrum.co.uk/home.asp
Career Legal	www.careerlegal.co.uk

City Jobs – Legal	www.cityjobs.com/search-legal.html
G2 Legal	www.g2legal.co.uk
Inside Careers – Patent Attorneys	www.insidecareers.co.uk/patent/index.htm
Interactive Lawyer.com	www.interactive-lawyer.com/ILrecr.html
Jobs for Lawyers	www.jobsforlawyers.co.uk
Jobs in Law	www.jobsin.co uk/law/
Law Society Gazette	www.lawgazette.co.uk
Law Lounge	www.lawlounge.com
Lawyer-At-Work.com	www.lawyer-at-work.com
The Legal Recruitment Company	www.legal-recruitment.co.uk
The Student Law Centre	www.studentlaw.com
The Lawyer	www.the-lawyer.co.uk
totally legal	www.totallylegal.co.uk

Manufacturing, production and procurement

Dyson	www.dyson.co.uk
Jimfinder.com	www.jimfinder.com
JobOil.com	www.joboil.com
Jobsin.co.uk	www.jobsin.co.uk
Jobs in Manufacturing	www.jobsin.co.uk/manufacturing/
Jobs in Utilities	www.jobsin.co.uk/utilities/
Oil Careers	www.oilcareers.com
Scotweld	www.scotweld.demon.co.uk

Miscellaneous

Jobs in Energy	http://www.jobsin.co.uk/energy/jobseeker.htm
AquariumJobs	www.aquariumjobs.co.uk
ENDS	www.ends.co.uk/jobs/
hrstaff.co.uk	www.hrstaff.co.uk
InHR	www.inhr.co.uk
Jobs Circuit	www.jobscircuit.co.uk
Jobs in Administration	www.jobsin.co.uk/administration/
Jobs in Fire	www.jobsin.co.uk/fire/
Jobs in Leisure	www.jobsin.co.uk/leisure/
Jobs in Prisons	www.jobsin.co.uk/prisons/

MBAjobsnet	www.mbsjobs.net
Mechanical Jobs	www.mechanicaljobs.com
Motor Careers	www.motor-careers.co.uk
Nanny Job	www.nannyjob.co.uk
OneWorld Jobs	www.nt.oneworld.org/jobs/
RecruitersOnline	www.recruitersonline.co.uk
SecsintheCity	www.secsinthecity.com
Inside Careers – Actuaries	www.insidecareers.co.uk/ actuaries/index.htm
Jobs in Insurance	www.jobsin.co.uk/insurance/
JustInsuranceJobs	www.justinsurancejobs.co.uk
Propertejobs.com	www.propertejobs.com
Purplemoves.com	www.purplemoves.com

Public sector and charity

Jobs in Government	http://www.jobsin.co.uk/ government/jobseeker.htm
Fast Stream, European and Recruitment Division	www.cabinet-office.gov.uk/fsesd/
CharityJob	www.charityjob.co.uk
Charity Recruitment	www.charityopps.com
Charity People	www.charitypeople.co.uk
Civil Service Recruitment Gateway	www.civilservice.gov.uk
UK Fundraising	www.fundraising.co.uk
Jobs4PublicSector.com	www.jobs4publicsector.com
Jobs Go Public	www.jobsgopublic.com
Jobs in Charity	www.jobsin.co.uk/charities/
Jobs in Police	www.jobsin.co.uk/police/
Jobs in Services	www.jobsin.co.uk/services/
LGCNet	www.lgcnet.com
The Museum Association	www.museumsassociation.org
Sector1.net	www.sector1.net
SocietyGuardian	www.societyguardian.co.uk
VSO	www.vso.org.uk

Retail and wholesale

Foodjobs	www.foodjobs.co.uk
foodmanjobs.co.uk	www.foodmanjobs.co.uk
GrocerJobs.com	www.grocerjobs.com

inRetail	www.inretail.co.uk
Jobs in Retail	www.jobsin.co.uk/retail/
Retail Careers	www.retailcareers.co.uk
Supermarketjobs	www.supermarketjobs.co.uk

Sales, marketing and advertising

Campaign	www.campaignlive.com
E-Job	www.e-job.net
Jobs in Sales and Marketing	www.jobsin.co.uk/ salesandmarketing
Jobs in Marketing	www.jobs-in-marketing.co.uk
mad.co.uk	www.mad.co.uk
Major Players	www.majorplayers.co.uk
Pareto Law PLC	www.paretolaw.co.uk
PR Week	www.prweekuk.com
SalesVacancies.com	www.salesvacancies.com
salesvacancies.com	www.salesvacancies.net

Science

Acumen	www.acumen.demon.co.uk
BioTech	www.biofind.com/jobs/
BioMedNet	www.biomednet.com
Bioscience Jobs	www.bioscience-jobs.com
Chemsoc Careers	www.chemsoc.org/careers/ careers.htm
CPL Employment Services	www.cplscientific.co.uk/ses/
Easyline	www.easyline.co.uk
First Science	www.firstscience.com
Green Channel Vacancies	www.greenchannel.com/jobs/
Information for Industry	www.ifi.org.uk
IPEM Enterprises Limited	www.ipem.org.uk/jobs/
John Innes Centre	www.jic.bbscr.ac.uk
Jobs in Science	www.jobsinscience.com
Naturejobs	www.naturejobs.com
New Scientist	www.newscientistjobs.com
Science's New Wave	www.nextwave.sciencemag.org
The Environment Post	www.pathcom.co.uk/ADC/
Pharmajobs	www.pharmajobs.co.uk
pharmavacancies.com	www.pharmavacancies.com

PhysicsWeb   www.physicsweb.org
Science Recruitment   www.science-recruitment.com
Tessella   www.tssp.co.uk

Telecommunications

British Telecom   www.bt.com
Commserve   www.commserve.co.uk
Cramer Systems   www.cramersystems.com
Energis   www.energis.co.uk
Jobs in Telecoms   www.jobsin.co.uk/telecoms/
Colt Communications   www.job-surf.com
Techcentria   www.techcentria.com
Telecomsnet.com   www.telecomsnet.com
Telecom Vacancies   www.telecomsvacancies.co.uk
telepeople.com   www.telepeople.com
T for Telecommunications   www.tfortelecommunications.
                                     co.uk

Transport, logistics and aerospace

Airline Recruitment Agency   www.airlineappointments.com
AirMech.co.uk Ltd   www.airmech.co.uk
Airline Maintenance Resources   www.aviationmaintenance.co.uk
FlyingTalent.com   www.flyingtalent.com
Jobs in Airport   www.jobsin.co.uk/airport/
Aerocontractor   www.aerocontractor.com
Airline Recruitment and Training www.artc.co.uk
   Company
AviationJobs   www.aviationjobs.com
Aviation Job Search   www.aviationjobsearch.co.uk
Inside Careers – Logistics   www.insidecareers.co.uk/
   Management   logistics/index.htm
Space Careers   www.spacelinks.com
Topshippingjobs.co.uk   www.topshippingjobs.co.uk

Travel and hospitality

Cater Jobs   www.caterjobs.co.uk
FoodJobs   www.foodjobs.co.uk

hcareers.com	www.hcareers.com
Hospitality Connnections	www.hospitalityconnections.co.uk
HotelandCaterer.com	www.hotelandcaterer.com
Hotelier	www.hotelier.co.uk
Hotel Jobs	www.hotel-jobs.co.uk
Jobs4chefs	www.jobs4chefs.com
Job Shopper	www.jobshopper.co.uk
Jobs in Catering	www.jobsin.co.uk / catering /
Jobs in Travel and Tourism	www.jobsin.co.uk / travelandtourism /
New Frontiers	www.newfrontiers.co.uk
Noel Recruitment	www.noelrecruit.ie / web / hotel.htm
The Food Site	www.thefoodsite.com
Travel Industry Jobs	www.travelindustryjobs.co.uk
Travel Tourism Jobs UK	www.ttjobs.com
Airline Appointments	www.uk-aa.com

8. Diversity

Age Concern	www.ace.org.uk
WSET Directory	www.ae.ic.ac.uk / wset / home.html
Association for Women in Science and Engineering	www.awise.org
Black Britain	www.blackbritain.co.uk
Society of Black Lawyers	www.blink.org.uk / organ / sbl.htm
BusinessFiles Online	www.businessfiles-online.com
British Women's Pilot Association	www.bwpa.demon.co.uk
Can Do	www.cando.lancs.ac.uk
EISE	www.comcarenet.co.uk / eise /
Commission for Racial Equality	www.cre.gov.uk
Daphne Jackson Trust	www.daphnejackson.org
Action on Age	www.dfee.gov.uk / age /
Disability Employment	www.disability-employment.com /
Disability Net	www.disabilitynet.co.uk
Disability Now	www.disabilitynow.org.uk / adverts.html
Employers Forum on Age	www.efa.org.uk
Specialist Services for the Disabled People	www.employmentservice.gov.uk / English / jobseekers / specialist_ services.asp
Equal Opportunities Commission	www.eoc.org.uk

EOP	www.eop.com
Fast Track Partnership	www.fast-trackpartnership.co.uk/
Fiftyon.co.uk	www.fiftyon.co.uk
fruitcamp.com	www.fruitcamp.com
GayWired.com	www.gaywired.com/ businessf2.cfm
homo.net	www.homo.net/classifieds/
icircle.com	www.icircle.com
kaleidoscopic.co.uk	www.kaleidoscopic.co.uk/ careers.htm
Gay and Lesbian Employment Rights	www.lager.dircon.co.uk
Workable workableuk	www.members.aol.com/
Number Ten	www.numberten.co.uk
Pakistani-Resource	www.pakistani-resource.org.uk
pinklinks.co.uk – jobs and careers	www.pinklinks.co.uk/Jobs_ Careers/Employment/
RainbowNetwork.com	www.rainbownetwork.com
Royal National Institute for the Blind	www.rnib.org.uk/
Women in Science, Engineering and Technology	www.set4women.gov.uk
Shaw Trust	www.shaw-trust.org.uk/
Skill	www.skill.org.uk
UK Black Links	www.ukblacklinks.com
Up and Running	www.up-and-running.co.uk
Ready, Willing, Able	www.website.lineone.net/ rwa/
Women's Unit	www.womens-unit.gov.uk
Women's Jobs	www.womenswire.com
Workforce	www.workforce.org.uk
Youreable	www.youreable.com

9. Corporate links

alljobsuk.com – major companies	www.alljobsuk.com/employers. shtml
Applegate Directory	www.applegate.co.uk
AskAlix	www.askalix.co.uk
BulkDirect	www.bulkdirect.com
Business.com	www.business.com
Companies House	www.companies-house.gov.uk

Monster.co.uk – Research Companies	www.company.monster.co.uk
corporate reports	www.corpreports.co.uk
Financial Times	www.ft.com
Hemscott.net	www.hemscott.com
Hoovers.com UK	www.hoovers.com/uk/
JobPilot – Companies	www.jobpilot.co.uk/ companyoverview/
London Stock Exchange	www.londonstockexchange.com
Millennium – UK Business Directory	www.milfac.co.uk
Scoot	www.scoot.co.uk
Silicon.com	www.silicon.com
The Internet Pages	www.the-internet-pages.com
Top Jobs – Company Profiles	www.topjobs.co.uk
Yell	www.uk.yell.com
UK Directory – Businesses	www.ukdirectory.com/cat-01
World Careers Network	www.wcn.co.uk
The Business Centre	www.web-centre.co.uk/ business.htm
Workthing –Who's Hiring	www.workthing.com/whoshiring/

10. Associations

AAT (Association of Accounting Technicians)	www.aat.co.uk
ACCA (The Assoc of Chartered Certified Accountants)	www.acca.co.uk
Association for Computers and Humanities	www.ach.org
The Institute of Actuaries	www.actuaries.org.uk
Advertising Association	www.adassoc.org.uk
Association for Outdoor Learning	www.adventure-ed.co.uk
Amalgamated Engineering and Electrical Union	www.aeeu.org.uk
Association of Learned and Professional Society of Publishers	www.alpsp.org.uk
Anatomical Society of Great Britain and Ireland	www.anatsoc.org.uk
The Royal Institute of British Architects	www.architecture.com

Association of Recognised English Language Services	www.arels.org.uk
Association for Science Education	www.ase.org.uk
Associations of Teachers and Lecturers	www.askatl.org.uk
Association of Secondary Teachers, Ireland	www.asti.ie
Association for the Teachers of Mathematics	www.atm.org.uk
The Associations of Taxation Technicians	www.att.org.uk
Association for University Teachers	www.aut.org.uk
British Association of Hospitality Accountants	www.baha-uk.org
British Association of Social Workers	www.basw.co.uk
British Association for Teachers of the Deaf	www.batod.org.uk
The British Computer Society	www.bcs.org.uk
British Dietetic Association	www.bdacareerchoices.com
The Institute of Safety in Technology and Research	www.bham.ac.uk/istr/homepage.html
The British and Irish Association of Law Librarians	www.biall.org.uk
British Interactive Multimedia Association	www.bima.co.uk/bimanetwork/jobs.htm
The Biochemical Society	www.biochemsoc.org.uk
Economic and Business Education Association	www.bized.ac.uk/ebea/
British Market Research Association	www.bmra.org.uk/bmra.html
The British Pharmacological Society	www.bps.ac.uk
Chartered Institution of Building Services Engineers	www.bre.co.uk
British BioGen	www.britishbiogen.co.uk
British Chauffeurs Guild Ltd	www.britishchauffeursguild.co.uk
British Web Design and Marketing Association	www.bwdma.co.uk
Confederation of British Industry	www.cbi.org.uk
Chartered Institute of Bankers	www.cib.org.uk
The Chartered Institution of Building Services Engineers	www.cibse.org
Chartered Institute of Marketing	www.cim.co.uk

Chartered Institute of Management Accountants	www.cima.org.uk
Chartered Institute of Building	www.ciob.org.uk
Chartered Institute of Personnel and Development	www.cipd.co.uk
The Chartered Institute of Purchasing and Supply	www.cips.org
CRAC	www.crac.org.uk/
The Royal Society of Arts	www.cs.mdx.ac.uk
Computing Services and Software Association	www.cssa.co.uk
Community Service Volunteers	www.csv.org.uk
Design and Technology Association	www.data.org.uk
European Council of International Schools	www.ecis.org
The Engineering Council	www.engc.org.uk
National Union of Journalists	www.gn.apc.org/media/nuj.html
International Associations of Teachers of English as a Foreign Language	www.iatefl.org
The Institute of Chartered Accountants of Scotland	www.icas.org.uk
Institution of Civil Engineers	www.ice.org.uk
Institute of Career Guidance	www.icg-uk.org
Institution of Chemical Engineers	www.icheme.org.uk
The Institution of Electrical Engineers	www.iee.org.uk
The Institute of Electrical and Electronics Engineers, Inc	www.ieee.org.uk
International Council of Scientific Unions	www.igpb.kav.se
Institute of Healthcare Management	www.ihm.org.uk
International Institute of Communications	www.iicom.org
International Institute for Environment and Development	www.iied.org
Institute for Learning and Teaching in Higher Education	www.ilt.ac.uk
The Institute of Mathematics and its Applications	www.ima.org.uk
The Institution of Mechanical Engineers	www.imeche.org.uk

Institution of Mining and Metallurgy	www.imm.org.uk
The Institute of Management	www.inst-mgt.org.uk
The Institute of Physics	www.iop.org
Institute of Practitioners in Advertising	www.ipa.co.uk
The Institute of Personnel and Development	www.ipd.co.uk
The Institution of Professionals, Managers and Specialists	www.ipms.org.uk
Institute of Public Relations	www.ipr.co.uk
Independent Schools Education Service	www.isis.org.uk
The Library Society	www.la-hq.org.uk
Wakefield & District Law Society	www.law-soc.co.uk
The Law Society	www.lawsoc.org.uk
The Law Careers Advice Network	www.lcan.csu.ac.uk/network/overview.htm
Association for the Teaching of Social Sciences	www.le.ac.uk/se/centres/ATSS/atss.html
London Investment Banking Association	www.liba.org.uk/
The Royal Society of Edinburgh	www.ma.hw.ac.uk/RSE/
The Mathematical Association	www.m-a.org.uk
Association of University Administrators	www.man.ac.uk/aua/
The Institute of Materials	www.materials.org.uk
The Royal Statistical Society	www.maths.ntu.ac.uk/rss/
The Biomedical Engineering Society	www.mecca.org/BME/BMES/society/bmeshm.html
AWCEBD	www.mistral.co.uk/awcebd
Motor Industry Training Council	www.mitc.co.uk
Montessori Centre International	www.montessori.ac.uk
National Association of Legal Secretaries	www.nals.org.uk
NATFHE	www.natfhe.org.uk
Professional Bodies (Education)	www.niss.ac.uk/world/prof-bodies.html
National Microelectronics Institute	www.nmi.org.uk
The Professional Association of Teachers	www.pat.org.uk
The Physiological Society	www.physiology.cup.cam.ac.uk
Political Studies Association	www.psa.ac.uk

London Mathematical Society	www.qmw.ac.uk/ lms/lms.html
Royal Aeronautical Society	www.raes.org.uk
Royal Institute of Architects in Ireland	www.riai.ie
Royal Incorporation of Architects in Scotland	www.rias.org.uk
The Royal Institute of Chartered Surveyors	www.rics.org.uk
The Royal Institution of Naval Architects	www.rina.org.uk
National Association for Coordinators and Teachers of IT	www.rmplc.co.uk/orgs/acitt/ index.html
The Royal Society	www.royalsoc.ac.uk
The Royal Society of Chemistry	www.rsc.org
The Society for the Promotion of Roman Studies	www.sas.ac.uk/icls/Roman
Standing Conference of National and University Libraries	www.sconul.ac.uk
Association of Art Historians	www.scorpio.gold.ac.uk/aah/
Staff and Educational Development Association	www.seda.demon.co.uk
Secondary Heads Association	www.sha.org.uk
Society of Information Technology Management	www.socitm.gov.uk
The Society of Medicines Research	www.socmr.org
SportsCoachUK	www.sportscoachuk.org
The Society for Research into Higher Education	www.srhe.ac.uk
NASUWT	www.teachersunion.org.uk
Teacher Training Agency	www.teach-tta.gov.uk
The Textile Institute	www.texi.org
Trades Union Congress	www.tuc.org.uk
Teachers' Union of Ireland	www.tui.ie
Association for Learning Technology	www.warwick.ac.uk
Irish Accounting and Financial Association	www.wit.ie/bussacc/iafa/ home.html
Guardian Unlimited	www.work.guardian.co.uk

11. Recruiters, appointment agencies and headhunters

Fish4Jobs – Recruiter Profiles http://jobs.fish4.co.uk/jobs/rec-now.jsp

Abatec Staff Consultants www.abatec.co.uk
About Jobs www.aboutjobs.co.uk
AbsoluteComms www.absolute-comms.co.uk
Aerotek www.aerotek.co.uk
Agency Central www.agencycentral.co.uk
Alljobs www.alljobs.ie
Agencies at alljobsuk.com www.alljobsuk.com/agencies.shtml

Employer's Recruitment Service www.amris.com
Apply4it.co.uk www.apply4it.co.uk
Aquent www.aquent.com
Advanced Resource Managers www.arm.co.uk
Astbury Marsden www.astburymarsden.co.uk
BakerHammond www.bakerhammond.co.uk/index.htm

BarclayAnderson www.barclayanderson.com
Beresford Blake Thomas www.bbt.co.uk
Best International www.best-international.com
bforbankingandfinance www.bforbankingandfinance.co.uk
Big-B.co.uk www.big-b.co.uk/jobs.html
Blue Fruit IT Recruitment www.bluefruit.co.uk
Boldly Go www.boldly-go.com
Border Personnel www.borderpersonnel.co.uk
Capita www.capita.co.uk
CareerCorner www.careercorner.co.uk

Contract Job Hunter – Online Recruiters www.cjhunter.com/contract.html
Contract Job Hunter – Directory of Online Staffing Firms www.cjhunter.com/dcsf/index.html
Recruiters at ClickaJob www.clickajob.com/other/recruit_comp.asp

Computer Futures www.computerfutures.co.uk
Computer People Online www.computerpeople.co.uk
ComputerStaff.net www.computerstaff.net
Corps Business www.corps.co.uk
Creative Recruitment www.creativerecruitment.co.uk
CRM People www.crm-people.co.uk
CRS Online.co.uk www.crsonline.co.uk

CV Screen	www.cvscreen.com
CV Search.net	www.cvsearch.net
Cyber-CV	www.cyber-cv.com
Dream IT	www.dream-it.co.uk
EAMES	www.eamesassociates.co.uk
Easy-Jobs.co.uk	www.easy-jobs.co.uk
Elan Computing	www.elan.co.uk
Beechwood Recruitment Limited	www.electronicjobs.com
Elliot Ross Associates	www.elliotross.co.uk
Welsh Nannies & Carers	www.epa.co.uk
Equilibrium Recruitment	www.eqrec.com
e-recruitnow	www.e-recruitnow.com
ESS Ltd	www.essltd.co.uk
Euronet Services	www.euronetservices.co.uk
Executive Select	www.executiveselect.co.uk
Executives Online	www.executivesonline.co.uk
First Person Global	www.firstpersonglobal.com
First Steps	www.firststepsltd.com
Futurestep	www.futurestep.co.uk
Top Agencies at Gis-a-Job	www.gisajob.com/gen/gold.htm
Goldensquare.com	www.goldensquare.com
Graduate Agency	www.graduate-agency.com
Greythorn	www.greythorn.co.uk
Harvard Associates	www.harvard-it.com
Harvey Nash Recruitment	www.harveynash.com
Haven Group	www.havengroup.co.uk
Hays Works	www.hays-ap.com
health-ejobs.com	www.health-ejobs.com
Heywood Associates	www.heywoodassociates.co.uk
Hi-Calibre Personnel	www.hi-cal.demon.co.uk
hunterhandley	www.hunterhandley.co.uk
Huxley Associates	www.huxley.co.uk
Integrated Communications Resource	www.icr-net.co.uk
IMR Recruitment	www.imr.uk.com
InRetail	www.inretail.co.uk
Directory-Jobs in the UK	www.ipl.co.uk/recruit.html
Recruitlink	www.iseeuk.f9.co.uk
IT Agency Ltd	www.itajobs.co.uk
IT Architects	www.it-architects.co.uk
IT Bods Ltd	www.itbods.ltd.uk
IT Executive	www.it-executive.com
IPTA Agency	www.itpa.co.uk

Just In Time	www.jitrecruitment.co.uk
Job Circles	www.jobcircle.free-online.co.uk
Jobline	www.jobline.co.uk
JobMall	www.jobmall.co.uk
Joboasis	www.joboasis.demon.co.uk
Jobs4u.com	www.jobs4u.com
Jobs Explorer	www.jobsexplorer.co.uk
Jobstaff	www.jobstaff.com
JobSurf	www.job-surf.com
Job World – NewMonday.com	www.jobworld.co.uk
JobZone UK	www.jobzone.co.uk
Jonas Consulting Ltd	www.jonas.co.uk
Jones Resourcing	www.jonesforjobs.com
Keillar Resourcing Ltd	www.keillar.com
Key Personnel	www.key-personnel.co.uk
Locum Group	www.locumgroup.co.uk
Manpower UK	www.manpower.co.uk
Masterlock	www.masterlock.co.uk
Matchtech Engineering Limited	www.matchtech.co.uk
Maya International	www.maya.co.uk
Mayday Recruitment	www.maydaygroup.co.uk
McGregor Muir (MM)	www.mcgregormuir.com
MediaTec	www.mediatec.co.uk
Meta Jobs	www.metajobs.net
Michael Page International	www.michaelpage.net
Monarch Recruitment	www.monarchrecruitment.co.uk
Multi Trak	www.multi-trak.co.uk
NES Online	www.nes.co.uk
Netjobs	www.netjobs.co.uk
Network Plus Recruitment	www.networkplus.co.uk
Newmarketingjobs.com	www.newmarketingjobs.com
Office Angels	www.office-angels.com
Opportunities Online	www.opps.co.uk
Outdoorstaff.co.uk	www.outdoorstaff.co.uk
Oxford Media	www.oxfordmedia.co.uk/ vacancies.htm
Pancake Promotions Limited	www.pancake.co.uk
ParkerMorse Associates	www.parkermorse.co.uk
Pathfinders Media Recruitment	www.pathfindersrecruitment.com
PermTemps	www.permtemps.co.uk
The Personnel and Care Bank	www.personnelcarebank.co.uk
PersonnelStore	www.personnelstore.com
PHDS Ltd	www.phds-jobs.co.uk

PlanetRecruit	www.planetrecruit.co.uk
Plastics Recruitment	www.plasticspeople.co.uk
PMR	www.pmr.co.uk
Progressive IT Recruitment	www.progressive.com
QE Recruitment Ltd.	www.qualityexpress.co.uk
React Recruitment	www.reactrecruitment.co.uk
Reed.co.uk	www.reed.co.uk
Roocruitment	www.recruiters.org.uk
Web Recruitment Directory	www.recruiters.org.uk
RecruitmentDatabase.com	www.recruitmentdatabase.com
Recruitment Revolution Ltd	www.recruitment-revolution.co.uk
Retailpersonnelservices	www.retailpersonnelservices.co.uk
RITS Consultants	www.rits.com
Roadhogs	www.roadhogs.com
round8	www.round8.com
Rugby Recruitment	www.rugbyrecruitment.co.uk
sceneone	www.sceneone.uk.com
Sci-Temps Ltd	www.scitemps.co.uk
Seltek Consultants	www.seltekconsultants.co.uk
Sharpstream	www.sharpstream.com
Shorterm Engineers	www.shorterm.co.uk
Silicon.com Recruitment	www.silicon.com
Beechwood Recruitment Limited	www.softwarejobs.co.uk
SportsRecruitment	www.sportsrecruitment.co.uk
Spring	www.spring.com
Stats Cole and Sharp	www.statscoleandsharp.com
Technicad Recruitment	www.technicadlimited.co.uk
Technical Recruitment	www.technical-recruitment.com
Scott Tatham & Co	www.technicon.co.uk
Telecoms Net	www.telecomsnet.com
TelfordJobs.co.uk	www.telfordjobs.co.uk
T for Telecommunications	www.tfortelecommunications. co.uk
LPA	www.the-lpa.co.uk
Liz Dargue Staffing	www.lizdargue.co.uk
The Network	www.thenetwork.co.uk
The Sportsweb	www.thesportsweb.co.uk
Top Jobs – Recruitment Advisors	www.topjobs.co.uk
Torres Partners	www.torres.co.uk
Towers Recruitment	www.towers.co.uk
TPA	www.tpa.co.uk
TPS	www.tps.co.uk
TravelRecruit	www.travelrecruit.co.uk

Trulink Appointments   www.trulink.co.uk
TSA Human Resources   www.tsa.co.uk
TMP Worldwide – UK   www.uk.eresourcing.tmp.com
Vision Recruitment   www.visionrecruitment.com
Victoria Wall Associates   www.vwa.com
Web Career Consultants   www.webcareer.co.uk
Worknet   www.worknet.co.uk
Workstream   www.workstream.co.uk
Workthing – Who's Hiring   www.workthing.com/whoshiring/
XR Recruitment   www.xr-recruitment.co.uk

12. Miscellaneous

Alec   www.alec.co.uk
AnalyzeMyCareer.com   www.analyzemycareer.com
BBC Knowledge: Work It Up   www.bbc.co.uk/knowledge/
    home/index.shtml
Career Talk UK   www.beta.communities.msn.co.uk/
CV writing   www.bradleycvs.co.uk
Buzzword   www.buzzwordcv.com
Career Exchange   www.careerexchange.com
Virtual Careers Library   www.careers.lon.ac.uk/links/
careersa-z.co.uk   www.careersa-z.co.uk
Careers Gateway   www.careers-gateway.co.uk/
    mainpage.htm
CareerShow   www.careershow.co.uk
Careersign   www.careersign.com
CareerSolutions   www.careersolutions.co.uk
Careers Portal   www.careers-portal.co.uk
CareerStorm   www.careerstorm.com
Careers Services National
    Association   www.careers-uk.com
Cendant Assignments
    International   www.cendantias.com
C Job Search   www.cjobsearch.co.uk
Connexions Card   www.connexionscard.gov.uk
Corporate Skills Ltd   www.corporateskills.com
CV Special   www.cvspecial.co.uk
Department for Education and
    Skills   www.dfes.gov.uk
Dumb Bosses   www.dumbbosses.com
Salary Search   www.e-commerce.uk.com

EuroJobs	www.eurojobs.com
Irish Job Page	www.exp.ie
Expats International	www.expats.co.uk
Expats Direct	www.expatsdirect.com
Expatriot Network	www.expatsnetwork.co.uk
The Weekly Telegraph	www.globalnetwork.co.uk
Guidance Enterprises	www.guidance-enterprises.co.uk
Hands On Solutions	www.handsonsolutions.com
hotrecruit.co.uk	www.hotrecruit.co.uk
IncomesData	www.incomesdata.co.uk
I-Resign.com	www.I-resign.com
JobRunner	www.jobrunner.co.uk
Job Search Monitor	www.jobsearchmonitor.com
JobsInWales	www.jobsinwales.co.uk
LabourMobility	www.labourmobility.com
Lifestyle UK	www.lifestyle.co.uk
Live In Jobs	www.livein-jobs.co.uk
Students as Entrepreneurs	www.livjm.ac.uk/careers/sae/hpage.htm
LocalWebGuide UK	www.localwebguide.co.uk
National Centre for Work Experience	www.ncwe.com
Overseas Jobs Express	www.overseasjobs.com
peopleculture.com	www.peopleculture.com
Reach for the Sky	www.reachforthesky.co.uk
SAT UK Recruitment Guide	www.recruit-online.co.uk
The Big Trip	www.thebigtrip.co.uk
The Blue Elephant Pages UK	www.theblueelephant.co.uk
Career Planning Homepage – Univ of Central Lancashire	www.uclan.ac.uk/dfee/career1.htm
UK Directory	www.ukdirectory.co.uk
Vacation Work	www.vacationwork.co.uk
Wideyes	www.wideyes.co.uk

Keywords

This keyword appendix is conceived to help you include in your CV some of the words that are frequently chosen by recruiters when they are using CV database software. Depending on the position and the profession, the recruiter chooses a selection of keywords that he or she feels best describe the desired capabilities and experience of the person sought. The software then searches the CV database for CVs that contain any of these words. Each document found is tabulated according to the number of times keywords selected by the recruiter appear. The CVs with the most 'hits' from the recruiter's selection rise to the top of the list.

You should use this keyword appendix as part of the editing process for building a really powerful CV. Once you have a draft that you feel packages your credentials and capabilities effectively, check it against both sections of keywords: **key verbs** and **key nouns**. As the verbs describe you in action and the nouns showcase that action happening in desirable areas, this is likely to improve the impact of your CV. Read the profession-specific nouns for your job and ask yourself, 'Have I done work in this area?' If the answer is yes, ask yourself, 'Is it in my CV?'

If you have experience in an area that is not in your CV, describe something you have done in this area. Your goal isn't to create a CV that includes lots of these keywords at the expense of an accurate description of your background. Rather it is to make sure your CV is the most powerful it can be, in ways that will get it pulled back from cyberspace and into the focus of a pair of human eyes – where it will most certainly impress.

Key verbs

Accepted	Controlled	Focused
Accomplished	Coordinated	Forecast
Achieved	Corresponded	Formulated
Acted	Counselled	Founded
Adapted	Created	Generated
Addressed	Critiqued	Guided
Administered	Cut	Headed up
Advanced	Decreased	Identified
Advised	Defined	Illustrated
Allocated	Delegated	Implemented
Analysed	Demonstrated	Improved
Appraised	Designed	Increased
Approved	Developed	Indoctrinated
Arranged	Devised	Influenced
Assembled	Diagnosed	Informed
Assigned	Directed	Initiated
Attained	Dispatched	Innovated
Audited	Distinguished	Inspected
Authored	Diversified	Installed
Automated	Drafted	Instigated
Balanced	Edited	Instructed
Budgeted	Educated	Integrated
Built	Eliminated	Interpreted
Calculated	Emended	Interviewed
Catalogued	Enabled	Introduced
Chaired	Encouraged	Invented
Clarified	Engineered	Launched
Classified	Enlisted	Lectured
Coached	Established	Led
Collected	Evaluated	Maintained
Compiled	Examined	Managed
Completed	Executed	Marketed
Composed	Expanded	Mediated
Computed	Expedited	Moderated
Conceptualized	Explained	Monitored
Conducted	Extracted	Motivated
Consolidated	Fabricated	Negotiated
Contained	Facilitated	Operated
Contracted	Familiarized	Organized
Contributed	Fashioned	Originated

Overhauled
Oversaw
Performed
Persuaded
Planned
Prepared
Presented
Prioritized
Processed
Produced
Programmed
Projected
Promoted
Proposed
Provided
Publicized
Published
Purchased
Recommended
Reconciled
Recorded

Recruited
Reduced
Referred
Regulated
Rehabilitated
Remodelled
Repaired
Represented
Researched
Resolved
Restored
Restructured
Retrieved
Revamped
Revitalized
Saved
Scheduled
Schooled
Screened
Set
Shaped

Solidified
Solved
Specified
Stimulated
Streamlined
Strengthened
Summarized
Supervised
Surveyed
Systemized
Tabulated
Taught
Trained
Translated
Travelled
Trimmed
Upgraded
Validated
Worked
Wrote

Key nouns

Administration

Administration
Administrative Infrastructure
Administrative Processes
Administrative Support
Back Office
Budget Administration
Client Communications
Confidential Correspondence
Contract Administration
Corporate Record Keeping
Corporate Secretary
Customer Liaison
Document Management
Efficiency Improvement
Executive Liaison
Executive Officer Support Facilities
    Management
Front Office Operations

Government Affairs
Liaison Affairs
Mail and Messenger Services
Meeting Planning
Office Management
Office Services
Policy and Procedure
Product Support
Productivity Improvement
Project Management
Records Management
Regulatory Reporting
Resource Management
Technical Support
Time Management
Workflow Planning/
    Prioritization

Association and not-for-profit management

Advocacy
Affiliate Members
Board Relations
Budget Allocation
Budget Oversight
Community Outreach
Corporate Development
Corporate Giving
Corporate Sponsorship
Education Foundation
Educational Programming
Endowment Funds
Foundation Management
Fundraising
Grassroots Campaign
Industry Association
Industry Relations
Leadership Training
Marketing Communications
Media Relations
Member Communications

Member Development
Member Retention
Member Services
Member-Driven Organization
Mission Planning
Not-For-Profit
Organization(al) Leadership
Organization(al) Mission
Organization(al) Vision
Policy Development
Political Affairs
Press Relations
Public Policy Development
Public Relations
Public/Private Partnerships
Regulatory Affairs
Research Foundation
Speakers Bureau
Special Events Management
Volunteer Recruitment
Volunteer Training

Banking

Asset Management
Asset-Based Lending
Audit Examination
Branch Operations
Cash Management
Commercial Banking
Commercial Credit
Consumer Banking
Consumer Credit
Correspondent Banking
Credit Administration
Credit Analysis
Debt Financing
Deposit Base
Depository Services
Equity Financing
Fee Income
Foreign Exchange (FX)
Global Banking
Investment Management

Investor Relations
Lease Administration
Letters of Credit
Liability Exposure
Loan Administration
Loan Processing
Loan Quality
Loan Recovery
Loan Underwriting
Lockbox Processing
Merchant Banking
Non-Performing Assets
Portfolio Management
Receivership
Regulatory Affairs
Relationship Management
Retail Banking
Retail Lending
Return On Assets
Return On Equity

Return On Investment
Risk Management
Secondary Markets
Secured Lending
Securities Management

Transaction Banking
Trust Services
Unsecured Lending
Wholesale Banking
Workout

Customer service

Account Relationship Management
Customer Communications
Customer Development
Customer Focus Groups
Customer Loyalty
Customer Management
Customer Needs Assessment
Customer Retention
Customer Satisfaction
Customer Service
Customer Surveys
Field Service Operation
Inbound Service Operation
Key Account Management

Order Fulfilment
Order Processing
Outbound Service Operation
Process Simplification
Records Management
Relationship Management
Sales Administration
Service Benchmarks
Service Delivery
Service Measures
Service Quality
Telemarketing Operations
Telesales Operations

Engineering

Benchmark
Capital Project
Chemical Engineering
Commissioning
Computer-Aided Design (CAD)
Computer-Aided Engineering (CAE)
Computer-Aided Manufacturing
  (CAM)
Cross-Functional Team
Customer Management
Development Engineering
Efficiency
Electrical Engineering
Electronics Engineering
Engineering Change Order (ECO)
Engineering Documentation
Environmental Engineering
Ergonomic Techniques
Experimental Design
Experimental Methods
Facilities Engineering
Fault Analysis

Field Performance
Final Customer Acceptance
Hardware Engineering
Industrial Engineering
Industrial Hygiene
Maintenance Engineering
Manufacturing Engineering
Manufacturing Integration
Mechanical Engineering
Methods Design
Nuclear Engineering
Occupational Safety
Operating and Maintenance (O&M)
Optics Engineering
Plant Engineering
Process Development
Process Engineering
Process Standardization
Product Design
Product Development Cycle
Product Functionality
Product Innovation

Product Lifecycle Management
Product Manufacturability
Product Reliability
Productivity Improvement
Project Costing
Project Management
Project Planning
Prototype
Quality Assurance
Quality Engineering
Regulatory Compliance
Research and Development (R&D)
Resource Management

Root Cause
Scale-Up
Software Engineering
Specifications
Statistical Analysis
Systems Engineering
Systems Integration
Technical Briefings
Technical Liaison Affairs
Technology Development
Test Engineering
Turnkey
Work Methods Analysis

Finance, accounting and auditing

Accounts Payable
Accounts Receivable
Asset Disposition
Asset Management
Asset Purchase
Audit Controls
Audit Management
Cash Management
Commercial Paper
Corporate Development
Corporate Tax
Cost Accounting
Cost Avoidance
Cost Reduction
Cost/Benefit Analysis
Credit and Collections
Debt Financing
Divestiture
Due Diligence
Employee Stock Ownership Plan
  (ESOP)
Equity Financing
Feasibility Analysis
Financial Analysis
Financial Audits
Financial Controls
Financial Models
Financial Planning
Financial Reporting
Foreign Exchange (FX)
Initial Public Offering (IPO)

Internal Controls
International Finance
Investment Management
Investor Accounting
Investor Relations
Job Costing
Letters of Credit
Leveraged Buy-Out (LBO)
Liability Management
Make/Buy Analysis
Margin Improvement
Merger
Operating Budgets
Operational Audits
Partnership Accounting
Profit Gains
Profit and Loss (P&L) Analysis
Project Accounting
Project Financing
Regulatory Compliance Auditing
Return on Assets (ROA)
Return on Investment (ROI)
Revenue Gain
Risk Management
Shareholder Relations
Stock Purchase
Strategic Planning
Treasury
Trust Accounting
Workpapers

General management, senior management and consulting

Accelerated Growth
Acting Executive
Advanced Technology
Benchmarking
Business Development
Business Re-engineering
Capital Projects
Competitive Market Position
Consensus Building
Continuous Process Improvement
Corporate Administration
Corporate Communications
Corporate Culture Change
Corporate Development
Corporate Image
Corporate Legal Affairs
Corporate Mission
Corporate Vision
Cost Avoidance
Cost Reduction
Crisis Communications
Cross-Cultural Communications
Customer Retention
Customer-Driven Management
Efficiency Improvement
Emerging Business Venture
Entrepreneurial Leadership
European Economic Community
   (EEC)
Executive Management
Executive Presentations
Financial Management
Financial Restructuring
Global Market Expansion
High-Growth Organization
Interim Executive
Leadership Development
Long-Range Planning
Management Development
Margin Improvement
Market Development

Market-Driven Management
Marketing Management
Matrix Management
Multi-Function Experience
Multi-Industry Experience
Multi-Site Operations Management
New Business Development
Operating Infrastructure
Operating Leadership
Organization(al) Culture
Organization(al) Development
Participative Management
Performance Improvement
Policy Development
Process Ownership
Process Reengineering
Productivity Improvement
Profit and Loss (P&L) Management
Profit Growth
Project Management
Quality Improvement
Re-engineering
Relationship Management
Reorganization
Return On Assets (ROA)
Return On Equity (ROE)
Return On Investment (ROI)
Revenue Growth
Sales Management
Service Design/Delivery
Signatory Authority
Start-Up Venture
Strategic Development
Strategic Partnership
Tactical Planning/Leadership
Team Building
Team Leadership
Total Quality Management (TQM)
Transition Management
Turnaround Management
World-Class Organization

Healthcare

Acute Care Facility
Ambulatory Care
Assisted Living
Capital Giving Campaign
Case Management
Certificate of Need (CON)
Chronic Care Facility
Clinical Services
Community Hospital
Community Outreach
Continuity of Care
Cost Centre
Electronic Claims Processing
Emergency Medical Systems (EMS)
Employee Assistance Program (EAP)
Fee Billing
Full-Time Equivalent (FTE)
Grant Administration
Health Maintenance Organization
   (HMO)
Healthcare Administrator
Healthcare Delivery Systems
Home Healthcare
Hospital Foundation
Industrial Medicine
Inpatient Care
Long-Term Care
Managed Care

Management Service Organization
   (MSO)
Multi-Hospital Network
Occupational Health
Outpatient Care
Patient Accounting
Patient Relations
Peer Review
Physician Credentialling
Physician Relations
Practice Management
Preferred Provider Organization
   (PPO)
Preventive Medicine
Primary Care
Provider Relations
Public Health Administration
Quality of Care
Regulatory Standards (JCAHO)
Rehabilitation Services
Reimbursement Programme
Risk Management
Service Delivery
Skilled Nursing Facility
Third-Party Administrator
Utilization Review
Wellness Programmes

Hospitality

Amenities
Back-of-the-House Operations
Banquet Operations
Budget Administration
Catering Operations
Club Management
Conference Management
Contract F&B Operations
Corporate Dining Room
Customer Retention
Customer Service
Food and Beverage Operations (F&B)
Food Cost Controls

Front-of-the-House Operations
Guest Retention
Guest Satisfaction
Hospitality Management
Inventory Planning/Control
Labour Cost Controls
Meeting Planning
Member Development/Retention
Menu Planning
Menu Pricing
Multi-Unit Operations
Occupancy
Portion Control

Property Development
Purchasing
Resort Management
Service Management

Signature Property
Vendor Sourcing
VIP Relations

Human resources

American Disabilities Act (ADA)
Benefits Administration
Career Pathing
Change Management
Chief Talent Officer (CTO)
Claims Administration
College Recruitment
Compensation
Competency-Based Performance
Corporate Culture Change
Cross-Cultural Communications
Diversity Management
Employee Communications
Employee Empowerment
Employee Involvement Teams
Employee Relations
Employee Retention
Employee Surveys
Equal Employment Opportunity
   (EEO)
Expatriate Employment
Grievance Proceedings
Human Resources (HR)
Human Resources Generalist Affairs
Human Resources Partnerships
Incentive Planning
International Employment
Job Task Analysis
Labour Arbitration
Labour Contract Negotiations

Labour Relations
Leadership Assessment
Leadership Development
Management Training and
   Development
Manpower Planning
Merit Promotion
Multimedia Training
Multinational Workforce
Organization(al) Design
Organization(al) Development (OD)
Organization(al) Needs Assessment
Participative Management
Performance Appraisal
Performance Incentives
Performance Re-engineering
Position Classification
Professional Recruitment
Regulatory Affairs
Retention
Safety Training
Self-Directed Work Teams
Staffing
Succession Planning
Training and Development
Train-the-Trainer
Union Negotiations
Union Relations
Wage and Salary Administration
Workforce Re-engineering

Human services

Adult Services
Advocacy
Behaviour Management
Behaviour Modification
Casework
Client Advocacy

Client Placement
Community Outreach
Community-Based Intervention
Counselling
Crisis Intervention
Diagnostic Evaluation

Discharge Planning
Dually Diagnosed
Group Counselling
Human Services
Independent Life Skills Training
Inpatient
Integrated Service Delivery
Mainstreaming
Outpatient
Programme Development
Protective Services
Psychoanalysis

Psychological Counselling
Psychotropic Medication
School Counselling
Social Services
Social Welfare
Substance Abuse
Testing
Treatment Planning
Vocational Placement
Vocational Rehabilitation
Vocational Testing
Youth Training Programme

International business development

Acquisition
Barter Transactions
Channel Development
Competitive Intelligence
Corporate Development
Cross-Border Transactions
Cross-Cultural Communications
Diplomatic Protocol
Emerging Markets
Expatriate
Export
Feasibility Analysis
Foreign Government Affairs
Foreign Investment
Global Expansion
Global Market Position
Global Marketing
Global Sales
Import
Intellectual Property
International Business Development

International Business Protocol
International Financing
International Liaison
International Licensee
International Marketing
International Subsidiary
International Trade
Joint Venture
Licensing Agreements
Local National
Market Entry
Marketing
Merger
Multi-Channel Distribution Network
Offshore Operations
Public/Private Partnership
Start-Up Venture
Strategic Alliance
Strategic Planning
Technology Licensing
Technology Transfer

Law and corporate legal affairs

Acquisition
Adjudicate
Administrative Law
Antitrust
Briefs
Case Law

Client Management
Contracts Law
Copyright Law
Corporate By-Laws
Corporate Law
Corporate Record Keeping

Criminal Law
Cross-Border Transactions
Depositions
Discovery
Due Diligence
Employment Law
Environmental Law
Ethics
Family Law
Fraud
General Partnership
Intellectual Property
Interrogatory
Joint Venture
Judicial Affairs
Juris Doctor (JD)
Labour Law
Landmark Decision
Legal Advocacy
Legal Research
Legislative Review/Analysis
Licensing
Limited Liability Corporation (LLC)

Limited Partnership
Litigation
Mediation
Memoranda
Mergers
Motions
Negotiations
Patent Law
Personal Injury
Probate Law
Risk Management
SEC Affairs
Shareholder Relations
Signatory Authority
Strategic Alliance
Tax Law
Technology Transfer
Trade Secrets
Trademark
Transactions Law
Trial Law
Unfair Competition
Workers' Compensation Litigation

Manufacturing asset management

Automated Manufacturing
Capacity Planning
Capital Budget
Capital Project
Cell Manufacturing
Computer-Integrated Manufacturing
(CIM)
Concurrent Engineering
Continuous Improvement
Cost Avoidance
Cost Reductions
Cross-Functional Teams
Cycle Time Reduction
Distribution Management
Efficiency Improvement
Environmental Health and Safety
(EHS)
Equipment Management
Ergonomically Efficient
Facilities Consolidation

Inventory Control
Inventory Planning
Just-In-Time (JIT)
Kaizen
Labour Efficiency
Labour Relations
Lean Manufacturing
Logistics Management
Manufacturing Engineering
Manufacturing Integration
Manufacturing Technology
Master Schedule
Materials Planning
Materials Replenishment System
(MRP)
Multi-Site Operations
Occupational Health and Safety
(OH&S)
On-Time Delivery
Operating Budget

Operations Management
Operations Reengineering
Operations Start-Up
Optimization
Order Fulfilment
Order Processing
Outsourcing
Participative Management
Performance Improvement
Physical Inventory
Pilot Manufacturing
Plant Operations
Process Automation
Process Redesign/Re-engineering
Procurement
Product Development and
    Engineering
Product Rationalization
Production Forecasting
Production Lead Time
Production Management
Production Output
Production Plans/Schedules
Productivity Improvement

Profit and Loss (P&L) Management
Project Budget
Purchasing Management
Quality Assurance/Quality Control
Quality Circles
Safety Management
Safety Training
Shipping and Receiving Operation
Spares and Repairs Management
Statistical Process Control (SPC)
Technology Integration
Time and Motion Studies
Total Quality Management (TQM)
Traffic Management
Turnaround Management
Union Negotiations
Value-Added Processes
Vendor Management
Warehousing Operations
Work in Progress (WIP)
Workflow Optimization
Workforce Management
World-Class Manufacturing (WCM)
Yield Improvement

Public relations and corporate communications

Advertising Communications
Agency Relations – Directed
Brand Management
Brand Strategy
Broadcast Media
Campaign Management
Community Affairs
Community Outreach
Competitive Market Lead
Conference Planning
Cooperative Advertising
Corporate Communications
Corporate Identity
Corporate Sponsorship
Corporate Vision
Creative Services
Crisis Communications
Customer Communications
Direct Mail Campaign
Electronic Advertising

Electronic Media
Employee Communications
Event Management
Fundraising
Government Relations
Grassroots Campaign
Investor Communications
Issues Management
Legislative Affairs
Logistics
Management Communications
Market Research
Marketing Communications
Media Buys
Media Placement
Media Relations
Media Scheduling
Merchandising
Multimedia Advertising
Political Action Committee (PAC)

Premiums
Press Releases
Print Media
Promotions
Public Affairs
Public Relations
Public Speaking
Publications
Publicity

Sales Incentives
Shareholder Communications
Special Events
Strategic Communications Plan
Strategic Planning
Strategic Positioning
Tactical Campaign
Trade Shows
VIP Relations

Purchasing and logistics

Acquisition Management
Barter Trade
Bid Review
Buy vs Lease Analysis
Capital Equipment Acquisition
Commodities Purchasing
Competitive Bidding
Contract Administration
Contract Change Order
Contract Negotiations
Contract Terms and Conditions
Cradle-To-Grave Procurement
Distribution Management
Economic Ordering Quantity
   Methodology
Fixed Price Contracts
Indefinite Price/Indefinite Quantity
International Sourcing
Inventory Planning/Control
Just-in-Time (JIT) Purchasing
Logistics Management

Materials Replenishment Ordering
   (MRO) Purchasing
Multi-Site Operations
Negotiation
Offshore Purchasing
Outsourced
Price Negotiations
Procurement
Proposal Review
Purchasing
Regulatory Compliance
Request for Proposal (RFP)
Request for Quotation (RFQ)
Sourcing
Specifications Compliance
Subcontractor Negotiations
Supplier Management
Supplier Quality
Vendor Partnerships
Vendor Quality Certification
Warehousing

Real estate, construction and property management

Acquisition
American Disabilities Act (ADA)
Asset Management
Asset Valuation
Asset Workout/Recovery
Building Code Compliance
Building Trades

Capital Improvement
Claims Administration
Commercial Development
Community Development
Competitive Bidding
Construction Management
Construction Trades

Contract Administration
Contract Award
Critical Path Method (CPM)
  Scheduling
Design and Engineering
Divestiture
Engineering Change Orders (ECOs)
Environmental Compliance
Estimating
Facilities Management
Fair Market Value Pricing
Grounds Maintenance
Historic Property Renovation
Industrial Development
Infrastructure Development
Leasing Management
Master Community Association
Master Scheduling
Mixed Use Property
Occupancy
Planned Use Development (PUD)
Portfolio
Preventive Maintenance
Project Concept-Driven

Project Development
Project Management
Project Scheduling
Property Management
Property Valuation
Real Estate Appraisal
Real Estate Brokerage
Real Estate Development
Real Estate Investment Trust (REIT)
Real Estate Law
Real Estate Partnership
Regulatory Compliance
Renovation
Return on Assets (ROA)
Return on Equity (ROE)
Return on Investment (ROI)
Site Development
Site Remediation
Specifications
Syndications
Tenant Relations
Tenant Retention
Turnkey Construction

Sales, marketing and business development

Account Development
Account Management
Account Retention
Brand Management
Business Development
Campaign Management
Competitive Analysis
Competitive Contract Award
Competitive Market Intelligence
Competitive Product Positioning
Consultative Sales
Customer Loyalty
Customer Needs Assessment
Customer Retention
Customer Satisfaction
Customer Service
Direct Mail Marketing
Direct Response Marketing
Direct Sales

Distributor Management
Emerging Markets
Field Sales Management
Fulfilment
Global Markets
Global Sales
Headquarters Account Management
High-Impact Presentations
Incentive Planning
Indirect Sales
International Sales
International Trade
Key Account Management
Line Extension
Margin Improvement
Market Launch
Market Positioning
Market Research
Market Share Ratings

Market Surveys
Marketing Strategy
Mass Merchants
Multi-Channel Distribution
Multi-Channel Sales
Multimedia Advertising
Multimedia Marketing
  Communications
National Account Management
Negotiations
New Market Development
New Product Introduction
Product Development
Product Launch
Product Lifecycle Management
Product Line Rationalization
Product Positioning

Profit and Loss (P&L) Management
Profit Growth
Promotions
Public Relations
Public Speaking
Revenue Growth
Revenue Stream
Sales Closing
Sales Cycle Management
Sales Forecasting
Sales Presentations
Sales Training
Solutions Selling
Strategic Market Planning
Tactical Market Plans
Team Building/Leadership
Trend Analysis

Security and law enforcement

Asset Protection
Corporate Fraud
Corporate Security
Crisis Communications
Crisis Response
Electronic Surveillance
Emergency Planning and Response
Emergency Preparedness
Industrial Espionage
Industrial Security
Interrogation

Investigations Management
Law Enforcement
Media Relations
Personal Protection
Public Relations
Safety Training
Security Operations
Surveillance
Tactical Field Operations
VIP Protection
White-Collar Crime

Teaching and education administration

Academic Advisement
Accreditation
Admissions Management
Alumni Relations
Campus Life
Capital Giving Campaign
Career Counselling
Career Development
Classroom Management
Conference Management
Course Design

Curriculum Development
Education Administration
Enrolment
Extension Programme
Field Instruction
Grant Administration
Higher Education
Holistic Learning
Instructional Media
Instructional Programming
Intercollegiate Athletics

Leadership Training
Lifelong Learning
Management Development
Peer Counselling
Programme Development
Public Speaking
Public/Private Partnerships
Recruitment

Residential Life
Scholastic Standards
Seminar Management
Student Retention
Student Services
Student–Faculty Relations
Textbook Review
Training and Development

Transportation

Agency Operations
Asset Management
Cargo Handling
Carrier Management
Common Carrier
Container Transportation
Contract Transportation Services
Customer Delivery Operations
Dedicated Logistics Operations
Dispatch Operations
Distribution Management
Driver Leasing
Equipment Control
Export Operations
Facilities Management
Fleet Management
Freight Consolidation
Freight Forwarding
Import Operations
Inbound Transportation

Intermodal Transportation Network
Line Management
Load Analysis
Logistics Management
Maritime Operations
Outbound Transportation
Over-The-Road Transportation
Port Operations
Regulatory Compliance
Route Management
Route Planning/Analysis
Safety Management
Safety Training
Terminal Operations
Traffic Management
Traffic Planning
Transportation Management
Transportation Planning
Warehouse Management
Workflow Optimization

How to find anything on the World Wide Web using search engines and Boolean logic

Think of the Internet as the world's largest library. Then imagine that library without the Dewey decimal classification system. There you are in a grassy field with 35 million books and you need to find just one fact, located on just one of the pages, in just one of those books... oh my. With hundreds of millions of Web pages online, you could literally spend a lifetime clicking from Web page to Web page to Web page. This is no laughing matter, as your time is very valuable. One of the biggest complaints about the Internet is that it is too difficult to find what you are looking for. The reality is that searching the Internet requires part skill, part luck and a little bit of common sense.

Fortunately, you do not have to attack the Internet alone. There are a number of free and useful online tools that can help with any search. These are called 'search engines' – and whatever you do, don't search the Net without them. There are literally dozens of free search engines, such as Google, Yahoo!, Lycos UK, Mirago and UK SearchEngine.com, just to name a few. The trick to successful searching is to understand how they work, so you can use the right tool for the job.

Search engines break down into three categories – directories, indexes and meta engines. Directories, such as Yahoo! and UK SearchEngine.com, are good at identifying general information.

In Figure A.1, you can see the categories that UK SearchEngine lists directly on its front page.

> **home page/front page** Every building you enter has a front door and entrance area. Together these help the entrant get a feel for the building. In a Web site, the front page or home page is the first thing you see when you arrive at the site. It is a front door that either lets you straight in or admits you through security with a password. The front page or home page also does duty as a shop window displaying all the yummy things you'll find inside.

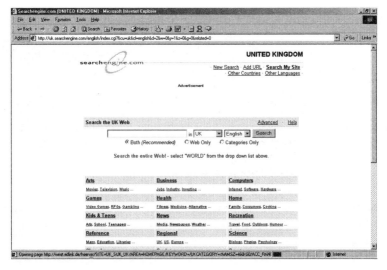

Figure A.1 A directory

The categories are the drawers of the site's card catalogue. Just like a card catalogue in a library, the site groups Web sites under similar categories, such as family travel, health and beauty shopping, and day trading. The results of your search will be a list of Web sites related to your search term or terms. If you are interested in locating the site for the National Gallery, for instance, use a directory (see Figure A.2).

But let's say you want more specific information, such as biographical information about Pablo Picasso. Web indexes are what you need, because they search the contents – the words – of an entire Web site. Indexes use software programs called spiders or robots that scour the Internet, analysing millions of Web pages and newsgroup postings, indexing all of the words.

Indexes like Mirago and Lycos UK find individual pages of a Web site that match your search, even if the site itself has nothing to do with what you are looking for. You can often find unexpected gems of information this way, but be prepared to sort through a ton of irrelevant information too.

Search results are usually ranked in order of relevancy – the number of times your search term appears in a document, or

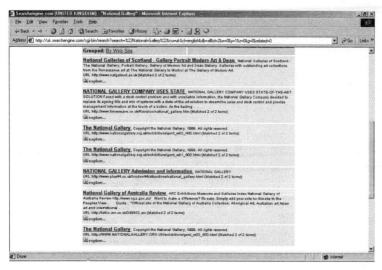

Figure A.2 Using a directory

how closely the document appears to match a concept you have entered. This is a much more efficient way to locate what you want – provided you have used the best concept or keywords to conduct your search.

In Figure A.3 we see the search results returned from Mirago, a UK index or keyword-based search engine. It returned 1,224 possible Web site matches. No one would want to view all 1,224 but, because of relevancy ranking, we can hope that some good sites are included in the top few. (This is similar to the recruiter reading only the top selections from the CV bank search.)

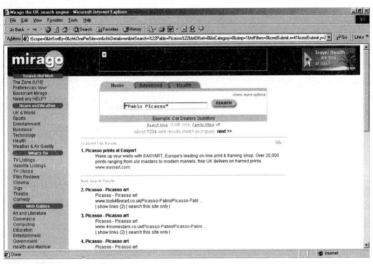

Figure A.3 A Web index

Meta search engines are our third type and, relatively speaking, the most recent. Meta engines search different search engines and return all the results to you. On the one hand, this sounds great – why go to all these different engines when one will do the work for you? On the other hand, you will lose effectiveness. Each search engine is a little different and you cannot expect the same search words and techniques to be effective on all sites. AllSearchEngines.co.uk (see Figure A.4a and b) is a great

Figure A.4a Using a meta engine to locate an employment site. You can clearly see the different search engines that the meta engine has gone through: Looksmart, Lycos and MSN.

Figure A.4b Having clicked on one of the sites listed, you are now straight into an employment agency's home page.

example of a meta engine and is a very powerful tool in its own right. As a starting place, a meta engine can be good, as it will tell you what search engines produced what results and you can then rely more heavily on specific engines that work well for you.

The exact syntax (the way the search engine sees each keyword or combination of keywords) each engine uses varies, so familiarize yourself with each engine's unique properties. By understanding how to perform sophisticated searches of online information, your chances of finding what you want will be greatly increased. Most search engines allow you to define your search criteria in very specific ways, but not all function the same way.

There are several types of syntax to consider, such as capital sensitivity, phrase searching, truncation and Boolean logic. Here is a quick overview of the different ways that these syntax types can affect your search results:

- Capital sensitivity. If a search keyword has an initial capital, the search engine will return only documents containing the word with an initial capital. For example, if you are interested in documents relating to the country China, capitalizing the word and using an engine that supports capital sensitivity will narrow down the number of results returned, eliminating documents that relate to china dishes or cookery. Note, however, that in many instances it is better to leave keywords uncapitalized to allow the engine to return results of documents that have keywords in either form.
- Phrase searching. When using search terms containing more than one word in a specific order, if you enclose the words in quotation marks the engine will return only documents containing all the words and *in that specific order*. For example, when searching for information on gun control, using 'gun control' will eliminate those documents which may contain the word gun and control but not in that order; possibly in entirely different paragraphs and maybe not even relating to gun control at all.
- Truncation. If you are looking for information on

gardening you may use 'gardening' as your keyword. However, if your results are limited in number (though not likely with gardening) and you want to broaden your search to get more results, you may use a root part of the word and abbreviate it with an asterisk ('garden*') so that the engine will return results of documents containing 'gardens', 'garden', 'gardener', 'gardeners', etc. In terms of your job search look at this possibility closely. For example, look at a very basic term such as 'management', 'manager', 'manage', 'managing', etc.

Boolean logic. This is the earliest of all searching techniques, developed by the English mathematician George Boole. It is a kind of logic, and has become the basis for computer database searches. Put simply, Boolean logic uses words called operators to determine whether a statement is true or false. The most common operators are AND, OR and NOT. These three words can be enormously helpful when doing online searches.

Perhaps the most useful feature in defining search criteria, Boolean operators can provide you with powerful control over the search engine logic. The Boolean operators AND, OR and NOT (or AND NOT in some engines) are in many ways analogous to mathematical operators like + and – in how they shape the execution of a complex equation. Some search engines will even accept the mathematical version in place of the words. Here's what these Boolean operators can do for you:

AND. If you are looking for a document that should contain all of your keywords, you can use the capitalized word AND between keywords (or, with some engines, you can use +) and the engine will only return documents that have both words. For example, using the search criteria 'Chelsea AND schedule' will return all documents that contain both words. Be sure to capitalize all letters in the word AND (or again, follow the site's instructions and use a +); otherwise the search engine will treat it as a keyword, not as an operator.

■ OR. If you want to broaden your search to find documents that contain either of the keywords, you can use the OR operator between words. This is very useful when searching for terms that have synonyms that might be used in a document instead. An example is 'children OR kids', which will return any document that has either of the words.

■ NOT or AND NOT. Using the capitalized AND NOT preceding a search term will eliminate documents that contain that term. Why might you want to do this? If you wanted to find information on fat-free recipes but did not want documents that include information relating to vegetarian recipes you could use 'fat-free recipes AND NOT vegetarian'.

The operators AND, OR and AND NOT are powerful in their own right but, when used in conjunction with parentheses, they offer substantial control over the search logic executed by the engine. Parentheses are used in Boolean logic similarly to the way they are used in a mathematical equation, limiting and ordering relations between variables. For example, if you wanted to find a Web-based Internet tutorial you might use the search criteria 'Internet AND (tutorial OR lesson)'. The documents returned must contain either both of the words 'Internet' and 'tutorial' or both of the words 'Internet' and 'lesson'. Essentially, the parentheses are used as they are for the distribution property in mathematics – to distribute the keyword 'Internet' to either of the two 'OR' words inside the parentheses.

There are many more uses of Boolean operators. Here are just a few more:

■ Parentheses. The most common use of parentheses is to enclose two possible keywords separated by an OR operator and then linking those enclosed or possible keywords with other criteria using AND. However, there are times and instances where the reverse arrangement might prove useful. For example, if you were looking for information on gun control you might want to use 'gun control OR (legislation AND gun)', which would return documents with the words 'gun control' or documents containing the word 'gun' and the word 'legislation'. You can further refine the search. Since the word 'law' is a synonym of 'legislation', you can nest one set of parentheses inside another to distribute gun to either 'legislation' or 'law' and, while you're at it, truncate 'law' with an asterisk to distribute 'gun' to the variations of 'law'. Here's how it would look: 'gun control' OR (gun AND (law* OR legislation))'. Note that each left-side parenthesis must be paired with a right-side one somewhere in the Boolean expression or the search engine will get confused.

- +require and – exclude. Some engines offer a variation of the Boolean operators AND and NOT. A + symbol preceding a word (with no space between) will require that the word be present in documents. A – symbol preceding a keyword will ensure that the word is not present in returned documents. Note that all words that must be in the document should be preceded by a + symbol, even the first word. For example, '+fraud +election' ensures that 'fraud' is in all the documents.
- Limited Boolean options. Some engines offer limited Boolean logic with radio buttons or pull-down menu choices such as 'All terms' (equivalent to using the operator AND between all terms), 'Any terms' (equivalent to using OR between all terms) and even date capability. Many search engines offer the ability to limit searches by Web page creation dates. This is a very useful tool for people who will be doing continuing research on a specific topic, enabling them to limit the results to pages created since their last search. It is also useful when searching for current event topics.

Figure A.5 shows an example of how a search engine can assist you with limited Boolean options.

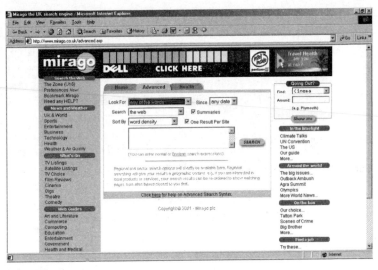

Figure A.5 Use of limited Boolean options

Remember, each search engine has its own unique short cuts and can be helpful in its own way. Personal preference plays a large role in determining what engine you like best. Beyond that, follow the instructions and truly analyse the words you utilize in your search. The more general the words you use, the more numerous and therefore non-specific (and possibly non-helpful) the results. Should you make your words and Boolean words too specific, you will get fewer results. Few results can also be an indication of the depth and scope of the search engine itself. So before you change your search techniques, try a different engine.

The search engines we used as examples in this text are UK-based organizations. Often, US and internationally based tools are more popular. For example, Yahoo! is one of the most popular search engines in the world. And the company is making every effort to customize Yahoo! UK to return geographically specific results. In some cases these international engines are tremendous resources, while in other instances a UK-based engine is best. Don't rule out any engine or technique. Be brave, experiment and have fun.

question index